ENGLISH TRANSFERWARE

Popular 20th Century Patterns

Joe Keller and Mark Gibbs

4880 Lower Valley Road, Atglen, PA 19310 USA

Dedication

Mark would like to dedicate this book to his mother, Jeanne Gibbs, for her love and support.

Joe would like to dedicate this book to David Daley and David Ross.

Acknowledgments

We would like to thank Mark's wife, Lucinda Gibbs, for her kind patience with the unending clutter and chaos that putting together the photographs for this book has entailed. Also, we would like to thank Pamela Konopka, David Ross, and Edward Hartung, and junior helpers Victoria and Alex Gibbs for their indispensable help with our photography sessions.

For their support of this project we would also like to thank: David Daley, Scott Differ, Douglas Congdon-Martin, Peter Schiffer, and the team at Schiffer Publishing.

We have tried to mention all those that helped with this project, but if we've overlooked anyone it is not from lack of appreciation. Thank you very much!

The photographs in this book are of pieces from the Gibbs family collection and from the inventories of Mark Gibbs or Joe Keller and David Ross.

Copyright © 2005 by Joe Keller and Mark Gibbs
Library of Congress Control Number: 2005931223

Covers and latout designed by: Bruce Waters
Type set in Korinna BT

ISBN: 0-7643-2348-2
Printed in China
1 2 3 4

Published by Schiffer Publishing Ltd.
4880 Lower Valley Road
Atglen, PA 19310
Phone: (610) 593-1777; Fax: (610) 593-2002
E-mail: Info@schifferbooks.com

For the largest selection of fine reference books on this and related subjects, please visit our web site at
www.schifferbooks.com
We are always looking for people to write books on new and related subjects. If you have an idea for a book please contact us at the above address.

This book may be purchased from the publisher.
Include $3.95 for shipping.
Please try your bookstore first.
You may write for a free catalog.

In Europe, Schiffer books are distributed by
Bushwood Books
6 Marksbury Ave.
Kew Gardens
Surrey TW9 4JF England
Phone: 44 (0) 20 8392-8585; Fax: 44 (0) 20 8392-9876
E-mail: info@bushwoodbooks.co.uk
Free postage in the U.K., Europe; air mail at cost.

Contents

The Scope and Organization of the Book

There are hundreds of companies that produced English transferware during the twentieth century and several thousand patterns. This book does not attempt to be comprehensive or representative. It does not provide histories of the English pottery manufacturers. Rather, we have decided to focus on those patterns that we consider to be the most popular. In our focus on patterns, we have gathered a wide variety of the items produced within the patterns, and assembled information on color varieties available and market values for various items, in the hope that collectors will find this information useful. Our most popular patterns are found in the first section of the book arranged alphabetically by pattern. The second section of the book includes a larger number of additional popular patterns. These are arranged alphabetically by manufacturer, and then alphabetically within company.

Both sections of the book contain our subjective conclusions on the popularity of patterns. We have no experimental basis for determining "popularity" other than our own experience. We have made several decisions to limit the scope of the book – the most obvious being that we have included only dinnerware that was produced in England during the twentieth century. While several patterns were introduced prior to 1900 and some are still in production, the focus of this book is the production during the twentieth century. We have also chosen to exclude most Blue Willow patterns due to scope and quantity of production and recommend other sources of information.

We have chosen to limit specific measurement information of many items and have opted to more general terms for a variety of reasons, including changes to moulds and product lines over long production history. Similarly, many patterns have undergone substantial changes that reflect changing market demands and styles. We have not attempted to be comprehensive in illustrating all of these changes.

Pricing

Establishing values for English Transferware has been especially difficult because of the wide spectrum of sources for pricing information. We have tried to create a market price that reflects an average price across this wide marketplace, taking into account specialist dealers' selling prices, on-line auction services results, replacement service prices, and general value as collectibles.

These transferware patterns were mostly mass produced and extremely popular. Some have been in production for nearly 200 years – so clearly several factors come in to establishing the value of any piece. First off, **condition** is extremely important. Prices in this book reflect pieces in excellent condition, with no chips, cracks, repairs, or damage. While minor age crazing is acceptable for many collectors, others demand pieces free of any sign of age or wear. Secondly, prices in this book are for **vintage** pieces only. The value of vintage items can be affected by current production and we have tried to take this into account, but we are not reflecting current retail price for contemporary items. Collectors should be aware of current production, backstamps, and retail price – as well as the presence of seconds in the marketplace. While the prices in this book are for vintage pieces, for some patterns (like Spode's Tower, with nearly two centuries of production) it is difficult to establish a price for any specific piece. A mid-nineteenth century flow blue dinner plate may be worth many times the value of a 1950s example. On the other hand, the 1950s plate that matches most dinner sets, may be the more saleable item. And finally, price is established by current **supply and demand**. Rare pieces in popular patterns can be extremely expensive – as can items that are popularly used by decorators. As a general rule, dinner plates are in extremely high demand, whereas cups and saucers are not.

The values in this book should only be looked upon as a guide. The collector should expect to pay more from dealers or replacement services that attempt to carry a large stock of items in an almost "open-stock" capacity than they would from an estate sale or local flea market. Collectors should also be aware that values fluctuate with trends and other market conditions. Ultimately, it is the job of the collectors to establish prices with which they are comfortable.

Introduction

During the eighteenth century, hand-painted blue and white Chinese export porcelain became the rage in England, and soon English potteries were struggling to compete in the expanding dinnerware market. In the late 1700s, Sadler and Green, Wedgewood, and other companies developed techniques for transferring prints to pottery. As time passed, English manufacturers perfected a variety of clay formulas for their dinnerware, and a variety of methods were developed to allow the transition from expensive hand-painted pottery to more mass-produced and affordable decorated dinnerware. Initially, English potters produced designs based upon the Oriental motifs found on Chinese export porcelain. In the early 1800s, however, a trend toward Western motifs, such as romanticized landscapes and still-life scenes with fruit and flowers, began to emerge. Many of these early designs either continued in production into the 20th century or served as an inspiration for the development of popular 20th century traditional patterns.

English transferware as a dinnerware category derives it name from its method of manufacture. The design is transferred not just once, but twice in the manufacturing process.

The early method of creating transferware involved a multistep process. First, an artist engraved the decorative design for a piece of pottery upon a metal plate, usually of copper. Next, the plate was heated on a stove, and then spread with ink. The excess ink was scraped off of the engraving plate, and a thin sheet of tissue paper sized with soft soap and water was placed over the engraving. The engraving plate and tissue paper were then passed through a press. Felt on the roller of the press forced the tissue paper into contact with every line and dot on the intricately engraved plate, transferring the design to the tissue paper.

The tissue paper print was then removed from the hot copper plate, and workers cut apart the various sections of pattern imprinted on the paper for use in decorating the pottery piece. While the ink was still damp, the thin tissue was carefully positioned on a previously fired piece of pottery and the image was again transferred, this time from the paper to the pottery, by rubbing it with a bristled brush lubricated with soft soap. The tissue paper was then washed off the pottery piece with cold water, and the piece was fired once to adhere the pigment to the object. Finally, an overglaze was applied to the pottery and it was refired, permanently preserving the image under a coating of clear glaze.

This process has been modernized and mechanized over the past two hundred years allowing for the mass-production of dinnerware.

We hope that the information in this book will be of value to a variety of interested parties: collectors of individual transferware patterns, collectors of items by specific manufacturer, collectors of specific transferware items (teapots or milk pitchers for example), and individuals or decorators using English transferware to decorate their homes.

A collection of transferware can give life to a curio cabinet, china cabinet, or Welsh dresser. In addition, assemblages of plates and platters displayed on a plate rail or hung on the wall in plate racks or individual plate holders can add vintage charm to most any room in the home.

Deco. Real Old Willow.

Part I: The Most Popular Patterns

Bristol – Crown Ducal

Crown Ducal's Bristol is a popular pattern with collectors. It is based on an early 19th century romantic transferware pattern called "Asiatic Pheasant." In the 1920s, a copy of the pattern was released under the trade name "Old Hall Ware." We conjecture that Crown Ducal purchased the rights to the pattern and took over its production under the pattern name "Bristol." The range of Crown Ducal backstamps found on individual pieces of the pattern suggests that it was in production from the 1930s until at least the 1950s. To date, we have not been able to discover any marketing materials or advertisements for this lovely pattern, but we have not given up hope!

Bristol can be found in five colors: pink, blue (a bright, vivid cobalt blue), grey-blue, purple, and greenish teal. Pink, blue, and purple are all equally popular with collectors, but thus far, there is much less demand for the grey-blue color, and lower market prices reflect this. The greenish teal shade in Bristol is extremely rare. The pattern is somewhat prone to crazing, and while mild crazing does not seem to matter much to most Bristol lovers, heavy crazing and/or staining adversely affects market values, especially for common pieces.

Contributing to Bristol's popularity is the wide variety of serving pieces available in the pattern. Multiple sizes and shapes of coffeepots and teapots are available, but getting harder and harder to locate in pristine condition. An especially large number of tea-related serving pieces appears to have been marketed in Europe. We continually "discover" new pieces, including a faststand covered marmalade jar, which we obtained too late to photograph for this edition of our book.

Bristol pink teapot $175-195, rectangular sandwich tray $145-165, small platter $75-85, fast-stand sauceboat $75-85, demitasse creamer $40-45.

Bristol pink dinner plate $30-35, salad plate $18-20, coupe plate $18-20, cup/saucer $18-20, cream soup with saucer $35-40, single eggcup $30-35, rim soup $18-20.

Bristol pink small oval vegetable $65-70, large oval vegetable $70-75.

Bristol pink relish/gravy liner $35-40.

Bristol purple coffee cup/saucer $22-25, salad plate $20-22, bread and butter $12-15, dinner plate $30-35, double eggcup $35-40, fruit bowl $12-15, teacup/saucer $18-20.

Bristol purple large platter $175-195, medium platter $120-130.

Bristol blue/grey dinner plate $18-20, salad plate $12-14, cup/saucer $15-18.

Bristol blue/grey sugar $40-45, oval vegetable $40-45.

Bristol blue demitasse cup and saucer $35-40.

Bristol blue/grey salt and pepper $45-50 pair.

Bristol backstamps. The "Old Hall Ware" backstamp is earliest; the crown logo is the latest.

Item	Pink	Blue	Purple	Blue/Grey
Bowl, creamsoup/liner	$35-40	$35-40	$35-40	$30-35
Bowl, fruit	$12-15	$12-15	$12-15	$8-10
Bowl, rim cereal	$18-20	$18-20	$18-20	$12-15
Bowl, soup coupe	$18-20	$18-20	$18-20	
Bowl, soup rim	$18-20	$18-20	$18-20	$15-18
Bowl, round vegetable	$60-65	$65-70	$65-70	$40-45
Bowl, oval vegetable small	$65-70	$65-70	$65-70	$40-45
Bowl, oval vegetable large	$70-75	$70-75	$70-75	$45-50
Bowl, covered vegetable	$160-175	$175-200	$175-200	$100-125
Butter dish, 1/4 lb.	$80-100	$90-100	$90-100	
Butter dish, round	$90-110	$100-120	$100-120	
Coffeepot	$175-200	$200-225	$200-225	$100-125
Coffeepot, demitasse	$175-200	$200-225	$200-225	
Creamer	$40-45	$40-45	$40-45	$30-35
Creamer, demitasse	$45-50	$45-50	$45-50	$35-40
Cup/saucer demitasse	$35-40	$35-40	$35-40	
Cup/saucer, coffee	$22-25	$22-25	$22-25	$18-20
Cup/saucer, tea	$18-20	$18-20	$18-20	$15-18
Eggcup single	$30-35	$30-35	$30-35	
Eggcup double	$35-40	$35-40	$35-40	
Marmalade, covered	$100-125			
Pitcher, 16 oz.	$90-100	$100-125	$100-125	$75-85
Plate, bread and butter	$12-15	$12-15	$12-15	$8-10
Plate, salad	$18-20	$20-22	$20-22	$12-14
Plate, lunch	$25-30	$25-30	$25-30	$18-20
Plate, dinner	$30-35	$30-35	$30-35	$20-25
Plate, handled cake	$90-100	$100-110	$100-110	$80-90
Platter, small	$75-85	$75-85	$75-85	$45-50
Platter, medium	$100-120	$120-130	$120-130	$60-70
Platter, large	$150-175	$175-195	$175-195	$90-100
Platter, extra large	$225-250	$250-275	$250-275	$175-200
Relish/sauceboat liner	$35-40	$40-45	$40-45	$30-35
Salt/Pepper				$45-50
Sauceboat, faststand	$75-85	$80-90	$80-90	$65-75
Sauceboat	$50-60	$50-60	$50-60	$40-45
Sugar, regular	$40-45	$45-50	$45-50	$40-45
Sugar, demitasse	$50-60	$50-60	$50-60	$35-40
Teapot	$175-195	$200-225	$200-225	$125-150
Tray, rectangular	$145-165	$145-165	$145-165	$90-100
Tureen, medium	$425-475	$450-500	$450-500	

Bristol blue large platter $175-195.

Calico – Royal Crownford, Burleigh

Calico is a single color, allover floral chintz pattern. It was produced from the 1950s until the 1970s by several English potteries. A good assortment of traditional place setting and serving pieces, as well as a wide variety of giftware and novelty items are available. At the height of the pattern's popularity during the 1950s, a number of Japanese go-along ceramic novelty pieces were imported. In addition, a group of tin items including canisters, trays, and lunchboxes were produced.

Calico is most often found in either dark cobalt blue or rich chocolate brown. In addition, Calico pieces have been reported in an avocado green. To date, however, green appears to have been used on giftware and novelty pieces only, with no standard place setting pieces having surfaced.

Blue Calico is the most popular color choice of collectors, and recently, Calico has been reissued in blue under the trademark "Queen's." Fortunately for collectors, new Calico is noticeably different from 1950s to 1970s production. First, it is important to note that so far, we are not aware of Royal Crownford backstamps having been reissued. Second, take notice that earlier English Calico pieces typically were produced on a relatively heavy, dense clay body, with a look and feel similar to vintage ironstone. In contrast, more recent reissues of the pattern appear on relatively lightweight china blanks which have a distinctively different feel from 1950s and 1960s production pieces.

Calico blue dinner bells $40-45 each, 6" plate $8-10, cup/saucer $15-18, cow creamer $75-85.

Calico blue bread and butter $8-10, dinner $22-25, cereal $8-10, cup/saucer $15-18.

Calico blue large milk pitcher $120-130, small octagonal platter $60-70,
vegetable bowl $50-60, salt and pepper $60-70 pair.

Calico blue creamer $30-35, teapot $160-175, cow creamer
$75-85, covered sugar $40-45.

Calico blue wash bowl
and pitcher $175-200.

Calico brown rim soup $15-18, small octagonal platter $50-60, dinner plate $18-
20, bread and butter plate $6-7, salad
plate $12-15, cereal bowl $8-10, 8" round
vegetable $40-50, cup/saucer $15-18.

Calico brown teapot $90-100, demitasse
open sugar $20-25, regular salt and pepper $45-50 pair, barrel salt and pepper
$60-70 pair.

Calico brown wash bowl and pitcher set $150-175, soap dish $22-26.

Calico brown sauce boat $40-45, liner $18-20, two spout fat-separator gravy $60-70.

Collectable Crownford backstamp and vintage Burleigh backstamp on heavy stoneware creamer.

Calico tin go-alongs. $20-45 each.

Castles – Enoch Wood's

Castles is an incredibly rich-looking scenic pattern. It is novel among scenic transferware patterns in that its border design does not merely encircle the center scene. Rather, the border frames each scene and forms a foreground of lush woodland trees and foliage.

Based on backstamps, it appears to have been manufactured primarily in the 1930s and 1940s. The pattern is most often found in vivid cobalt blue, but is most popular in purple. Castles is also occasionally found in pink.

Each piece of china within the pattern bears a specific castle scene or scenes. All dinner plates, for example depict Stokesay, while all cream soups and liners show Ross and Caerphilly respectively. The name of each castle depicted is included as part of the backstamp on each piece. A partial listing of pieces available and their respective castle engravings is as follows:

Item	Castle Scene
Dinner Plate	Stokesay
Salad Plate	Rubens
Bread and Butter	Caerphilly
Rim Fruit Bowl	Broughton
Coupe Soup Bowl	Dalguise
Cream Soup Bowl	Ross
Cream Soup Liner	Caerphilly
Small Platter	Chepstow
Medium Platter	Bodiam
Relish	Pengersick
Sugar Bowl	Manorbier
Creamer	Blarney
Teacup	Ross
Tea Saucer	Harlech
Oval Vegetable Bowl	Ludlow
Dutch Jug	Mostar

Castles blue bread and butter plate $12-15, dinner plate $30-35, salad plate $18-20, cup and saucer $18-20.

Castles blue rim fruit bowl $12-15, rim cereal bowl $18-20..

Castles blue round vegetable $65-75, oval vegetable $65-75, medium platter $100-125,.

Castles blue fast-stand gravy $75-85, butter dish $100-110, medium pitcher $100-125.

Castles creamer $40-45, teapot $175-195, covered sugar $50-60.

Castles blue relish $35-40.

Castles purple salad plate $30-35, dinner plate $40-45, creamsoup/saucer $45-50, coupe soup $35-40, bread and butter plate $18-20, cup/saucer $25-30.

Castles purple oval vegetable $90-100, medium platter $140-160, small platter $100-110, relish $45-50, covered sugar $60-65, creamer $45-50.

Castles large purple Dutch jug $120-130.

Castles pink jumbo cup and saucer $40-45.

Item	Blue	Purple	Pink
Bowl, fruit	$12-15	$18-20	$12-15
Bowl, cereal	$18-20	$18-20	$15-18
Bowl, creamsoup/liner	$40-45	$45-50	$40-45
Bowl, coupe soup	$15-18	$35-40	$15-18
Bowl, rim soup	$18-20	$30-35	$18-20
Bowl, 8" round vegetable	$65-75	$90-100	$65-75
Bowl, oval vegetable	$65-75	$90-100	$65-75
Butter	$100-110	$130-150	$100-110
Creamer	$40-45	$45-50	$40-45
Cup/saucer, regular	$18-20	$25-30	$20-25
Cup/saucer, jumbo	$40-45	$60-70	$40-45
Eggcup, double	$40-45	$45-50	$40-45
Pitcher	$100-125	$120-130	$120-130
Plate, 6" bread and butter	$12-15	$18-20	$15-18
Plate, 7" dessert	$18-20	$20-25	$18-20
Plate, 8" salad	$18-20	$30-35	$20-25
Plate, 9" lunch	$30-35	$35-40	$30-35
Plate, 10" dinner	$30-35	$40-45	$35-40
Plate, crescent salad	$40-50	$50-60	$45-50
Plate, chop	$120-130	$140-160	$130-150
Platter, small	$75-85	$100-110	$90-100
Platter, medium	$100-125	$140-160	$130-150
Platter, large	$175-200	$200-225	$175-200
Platter, 18" extra large	$200-225	$225-250	$200-225
Relish tray	$35-40	$60-70	$50-60
Sauceboat	$75-85	$90-100	$75-85
Sauceboat, fast-stand	$75-85	$100-125	$90-100
Sugar	$50-60	$60-65	$50-60
Teapot	$175-195	$200-225	$175-195

Castles backstamp.

Charlotte – Royal Staffordshire, Royal Crownford

Charlotte is a delicate floral basket design translated to china tableware by world famous English ceramicist Clarice Cliff in the 1940s for Royal Staffordshire Ceramics. While at a glance the pattern seems to be uniform across all pieces, upon closer inspection it is apparent that each piece displays a different ornate basket with its own unique floral arrangement.

Charlotte can be found in blue, pink, purple, and brown. The pattern also appears in brown transfer printing with multicolored hand tinting of the floral arrangements. While lovely, this variation of the pattern is scarce and not so avidly sought as the other colorways. From a market value standpoint, purple and pink Charlotte command the highest prices, with pink being somewhat scarce on the market. Pink and purple prices are followed closely by brown prices. While brown Charlotte is currently just as popular as pink and purple, there seems to be a better supply of this color on the market, and prices for brown have not reached the pink/purple level.

Charlotte is especially lovely in blue, with the blue coloration taking on a soft, Williamsburg-like shade. Since pink, purple, and brown patterns are currently more popular, the blue Charlotte is available at "bargain" prices.

While Royal Staffordshire produced only basic place setting and serving pieces for their Charlotte dinner services, a substantial number of novelty items and accessories in the Charlotte pattern were produced by Royal Crownford and other English potteries. A number of vases, creamer and sugar sets, novelty teapots, and even a full Victorian-style toilet set with washbowl and pitcher, chamber pot, toothbrush holder, tumbler and soap dish were made.

Charlotte (Clarice Cliff) blue fruit $6-7, dinner plate $18-20, salad plate $12-15, rim soup $15-18, cup/saucer $15-18.

Charlotte (Royal Crownford) blue cube teapot $75-90.

Charlotte (Clarice Cliff) small platter $45-50, covered vegetable bowl $120-130.

Charlotte (Royal Crownford)
blue cow creamer $60-70.

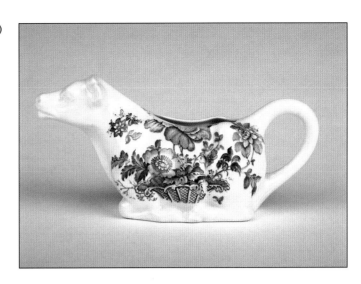

Charlotte (Royal Crownford) blue
bud vases $40-45 each, individual
sauceboat and liner $30-35..

Charlotte (Meakin) blue large milk pitcher
$80-90, small milk pitcher $65-75.

Charlotte (Clarice Cliff) pink medium platter $120-130, dinner plate $30-35.

Charlotte (Meakin) pink milk jug $75-90.

Charlotte (Royal Crownford) pink dinner bell $50-60, 3-cup dry measure $75-85.

Charlotte (Royal Crownford) pink demitasse cup/saucer $35-40.

Charlotte (Clarice Cliff) purple rim soup $18-20, salad plate $18-20, dinner plate $30-35, cereal $15-18, fruit $12-15, cup/saucer $18-20, bread and butter plate $12-15.

Charlotte (Clarice Cliff) purple fast-stand gravy $75-85, creamer $40-45, covered sugar $50-60.

Charlotte (Clarice Cliff) brown rim soup $18-20, dinner plate $20-25, bread and butter plate $8-10.

Charlotte (Royal Crownford) brown demitasse creamer $25-30, demitasse sugar $35-40, ashtray $20-25, cheese wedge $110-120.

Charlotte (Royal Crownford) dinner bell $50-60, pinch bud vase $60-70, cow creamer $60-70.

Charlotte brown vases $40-45 each.

Backstamps of vases showing two different companies for similar pieces.

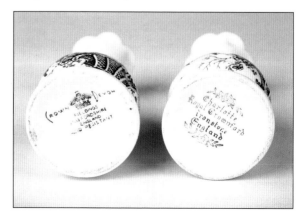

Charlotte (Clarice Cliff)
brown leaf dish $50-60.

Charlotte (Meakin) brown milk pitcher $65-75.

Charlotte (Royal Crownford) brown novelty mug $30-35.

Charlotte (Clarice Cliff) brown 5" Jack-in-the-pulpit wall pocket $90-100.

Charlotte (Meakin) Individual wash bowl and pitcher set $90-100.

 Charlotte (Royal Crownford) brown tumbler $30-35, soap dish $30-35, chamber pot $50-60.

Charlotte (Wilkinson) Light switch plate $75-90
with Wilkinson backstamp.

Charlotte (Clarice Cliff)
brown multicolored rim
soup $18-20.

Charlotte (Royal Crownford) brown multi-color miniature pitcher $20-25.

Charlotte Royal Crownford backstamp.

Charlotte Clarice Cliff backstamp.

English Chippendale – Johnson Brothers

A perennial favorite with collectors, Johnson Brothers produced English Chippendale from the 1930s until the mid-1960s. The design appears to be based upon an 18th century textile or wallpaper engraving. The pattern is found most often in pink, and less frequently in bright blue, with market prices for these two colors being comparable. Occasionally, one can find English Chippendale pieces in a lovely bluish-green or teal shade. While scarce, the teal colorway is not so popular as its pink and blue counterparts, therefore market values for teal are low.

A vast number of pieces are available to English Chippendale collectors with the patience to seek them out! Place setting pieces include 9" luncheon plates, 7" sandwich or dessert plates, coffee cups and saucers, teacups and saucers, jumbo cups and saucers, demitasse cups and saucers…etc.!

Two different soup tureen shapes have been found. The smaller of the two soup tureens is shaped just like a giant version of the sugar bowl, an overall rectangular shape with four small feet at the base. The larger version of the soup tureen is also rectangular, but has a pedestal-style base, rather than individual feet.

It is interesting to note that while coffeepots are fairly readily available in English Chippendale, teapots are especially hard to find in mint condition. Almost every teapot we encounter has a chipped spout or foot or has heavy crazing and staining. Apparently, those who chose English Chippendale as their china pattern must have used their teapots often!

English Chippendale pink rim cereal bowl $14-16, fruit $8-10, square salad plate $18-20, bread and butter plate $6-7, dinner plate $18-20, cup/saucer $15-18, jumbo cup/saucer $30-35, double eggcup $30-35.

English Chippendale pink oval vegetable $40-45, sauceboat $40-45, small platter $50-60, large platter $90-100, covered toast $100-125, demi-tasse sugar $45-50, regular creamer $30-35.

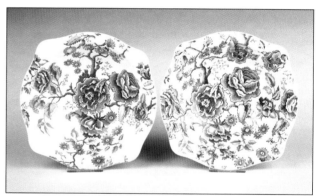

English Chippendale pink round vegetable (2 transfer variations, left is abnormal) $35-40 each.

English Chippendale pink large soup tureen $425-475.

Item	Pink/Blue	Item	Pink/Blue
Bowl, fruit rim	$6-7	Pitcher, medium Dutch	$60-70
Bowl, fruit coupe	$8-10	Pitcher, large	$75-85
Bowl, cereal tab	$14-16	Plate, bread and butter	$6-7
Bowl, cereal rim	$14-16	Plate, dessert	$6-7
Bowl, soup rim	$15-18	Plate, round salad	$12-14
Bowl, soup coupe	$14-16	Plate, square salad	$18-20
Bowl, creamsoup/liner	$30-35	Plate, lunch	$18-20
Bowl, round vegetable	$35-40	Plate, dinner	$18-20
Bowl, lg round veg.	$40-45	Plate, hostess w/cup	$20-25
Bowl, oval vegetable	$40-45	Plate, chop	$100-110
Bowl, cov. veg. rectangular	$100-120	Platter, small	$50-60
Bowl, cov. veg round	$100-120	Platter, medium	$65-75
Coffeepot	$150-175	Platter, large	$90-100
Creamer, regular	$30-35	Relish/sauceboat liner	$30-35
Creamer, demitasse	$30-35	Sauceboat	$40-45
Cup/saucer, regular	$15-18	Sauceboat, fast stand	$75-85
Cup/saucer, demitasse	$24-26	Sugar, regular	$40-45
Cup/saucer, jumbo	$30-35	Sugar, demitasse covered	$45-50
Cup/saucer, joke large	$150-175	Sugar, demitasse open	$40-45
Eggcup, double	$40-45	Teapot	$300-350
Ginger Jar	$100-125	Toast, covered	$100-125
Mugs (several styles)	$18-20	Tureen, 2 sizes	$425-475
Pitcher, small	$40-50	Waste bowl	$45-50

English Chippendale backstamp from large soup tureen.

English Chippendale teal eggcup $30-35.

English Chippendale blue dinner plate $18-20, round salad plate $12-14, fruit $6-7.

English Scenery – Enoch Wood's

English Scenery is a lovely scenic pattern produced by Enoch Wood's from the 1930s to the 1950s on smooth-edged blanks. It appears that Wood's reissued the pattern on swirled (as opposed to smooth) blanks sometime in the 1960s with production most likely continuing into the 1970s. English Scenery is found in blue, pink, purple, sienna brown with multicolored tinting, and infrequently, in dark brown with multicolored tinting.

In addition to the regular English scenery line, Wood's manufactured special Thanksgiving sets consisting of a large 20 inch platter and 12 full-sized dinner or "buffet" plates using the English Scenery border, but substituting turkey scenes for the standard pastoral center scenes. These Thanksgiving sets have been found in blue, blue with multicolored tinting, pink, sienna brown, and sienna brown with multicolored tinting.

English Scenery offers the collector a wide selection of both place setting and serving pieces from which to choose. Occasionally, small square dessert or sandwich plates are found. These appear to have been marketed as a sandwich set including six square plates and the rectangular handled sandwich tray. There are also extremely scarce octagonal luncheon plates available. Within serving pieces, there are at least three different shapes available for teapots and coffeepots. Moreover, all teapot and coffeepot shapes were made in multiple sizes! Keep your eye out for novelty pieces as well. One collector has reported a spoon rest as well an English "cruet" consisting of a tray with built in salt dip, pepper shaker, and mustard pot. Only time will tell what other English Scenery items will surface.

English Scenery blue salad plate $18-20, bread and butter plate $8-10, dinner plate $22-25, square 6" plate $24-26.

English Scenery blue lunch plate $20-22, round handled cake plate $90-100, salad plate $18-20.

English Scenery blue medium pitcher $75-85, coffeepot $125-150, large teapot $150-175, medium teapot $125-150.

English Scenery blue oval vegetable $50-60, jumbo cup/saucer $35-40.

English Scenery blue creamsoup with liner $30-35, large turkey platter (regular center) $200-225.

English Scenery blue large
soup tureen $350-400,
chop plate $100-110.

English Scenery later swirled blue sauceboat and liner $40-45, green salad plate $10-12.

English Scenery pink small platter $75-85, octagonal lunch plate $60-70.

English Scenery pink individual jelly/master salt $22-25, coaster $18-20.

English Scenery pink bread and butter plate $12-15, dinner plate $30-35, lunch plate $25-30, salad plate $18-20, crescent salad $50-60, jumbo cup/saucer $40-45, regular cup/saucer $18-20.

English Scenery pink rectangular celery tray $100-110, square handled cake $120-130, medium oval vegetable $60-65, large oval vegetable $65-75.

English Scenery pink medium platter $100-110, covered vegetable "potato" dish $130-150.

English Scenery pink salt and pepper $75-85 pair.

English Scenery pink turkey plate $50-60.

English Scenery pink creamer $35-40, fast-stand gravy $75-85, chocolate pot $200-225, "transitional" teapot $150-175.

English Scenery brown multi-color salad plate $18-20, large platter $100-125, double eggcup $30-35, demitasse cup/saucer $18-20.

English Scenery brown multi-color. Dark brown hostess plate with cup indent $22-25, dinner plate $20-25.

English Scenery backstamp.

English Scenery purple dinner plate $35-40, oval vegetable bowl $75-85.

Friendly Village – Johnson Brothers

Friendly Village has been in continuous production since the pattern was designed in the early 1950s. According to a vintage Johnson Brothers advertisement, "'Friendly Village' is a nostalgic pattern depicting 16 different scenes in a small American country town." Various scenes in the pattern are unified by a grape leaf border, with the transfer printed in a brownish-green color, and then tinted by hand. "Soft, muted tones of brown, green, yellow, red and blue capture the natural colors of the seasons evoking pleasant memories of simple rural life," the brochure goes on to explain.

In addition to the standard 10" dinner plate depicting "The School House," a series of 11" buffet plates were produced using twelve of the pattern scenes. The following table lists these twelve buffet plate scenes and a sampling of the other pieces upon which they appear..

Scene	Items
The Village Street	Coaster (Spring), Jumbo Cup
Autumn Mists	Round Vegetable Bowl
The Covered Bridge	Square Salad Plate, Square Coupe Soup, Square Coupe Cereal, Large (16") Platter, Covered Vegetable Bowl, Punch Bowl, Mug
The Hay Field	Small (11") Platter
The Lily Pond	Covered Sugar
The Old Mill	Round Cereal Bowl, Creamer, Coaster (Summer)
The School House	Dinner Plate
The Stone Wall	Fruit Bowl, Coaster (Autumn)
Sugar Maples	Bread and Butter Plate, Coaster (Winter), Tea pot
The Village Green	Small (12") Platter, Oval Vegetable Bowl
The Well	Relish or Sauceboat Liner
Willow by the Brook	Rim Soup Bowl

Over the years, Johnson Brothers has continued to add items to the Friendly Village pattern. In recent years, they have introduced a plethora of novelty serving pieces, and marketed go-along items such as cookware and linens. They've even added special scenes for Thanksgiving, and produced a line of Christmas items by using the center scene from the pattern, "Merry Christmas," with the Friendly Village border treatment.

Earlier, hand-tinted pieces are backstamped with the same brownish-green as the basic pattern, while more recent backstamps are printed in teal or black, and occasionally indicate that the item is "microwave safe."

Friendly Village round salad plate $10-12, square salad plate $12-14, dinner plate $15-18, double eggcup $22-25, regular cup/saucer $10-12, bread and butter plate $4-5, jumbo cup/saucer $24-26.

Friendly Village square coupe soup $12-15, rim soup $15-20, round cereal $7-10, round coupe soup/
small vegetable bowl $20-25, fruit bowl $5-6, square cereal $7-9.

Friendly Village small vegetable bowl $20-25, large round vegetable $20-25,
oval vegetable $20-25, covered vegetable $65-75.

Friendly Village small oval platter $22-25 large oval platter $40-45, medium oval
platter $30-35, relish/sauceboat liner $20-25.

Friendly Village turkey platter $125-150.

Friendly Village new platter. Notice changed shape and amount of undecorated space.

Friendly Village large soup tureen with ladle $250-275.

Friendly Village covered sugar $22-25, creamer $15-18, coffeepot $90-100, teapot $90-100, demitasse creamer $18-20, demitasse sugar $20-25.

Friendly Village sauceboat $20-25, liner $20-25, 14" chop plate $75-85, round soup tureen $175-200.

Friendly Village Dutch jugs/creamers. Regular creamer $15-18, demitasse creamer $18-20, medium jug $40-45, large jug $50-60.

Friendly Village quarter-pound butter $35-40, round butter/cheese dish $50-60.

Friendly Village mug $12-15, waste bowl $30-35, Christmas tree relish $40-45, salt and pepper $30-35, square hostess set $18-20.

Friendly Village Punch bowl $175-200, punch cups $18-20 each.

Friendly Village coasters $5-6 each. Far right coaster is not standard production. NV.

Friendly Village 2-tier tidbit tray $35-40 with original box.

Friendly Village buffet plates $18-20 each.

Friendly Village new buffet plate with turkey.

Friendly Village candlesticks with original box $75-85 pair.

Friendly Village backstamps. Brownish green mailbox is vintage; blue mailbox and "microwave safe" backstamps are in current production.

Historic America – Johnson Brothers

Historic America was introduced by Johnson Brothers in 1939 and produced until the early 1970s. The pattern consists of over 30 American scenes from 19th century engravings unified by an oak leaf and acorn border copied from an early 19th century transferware pattern.

Historic America was produced in blue, pink, and brown with multicolored tinting. Today's collectors most avidly seek the pink and brown multicolored versions of the pattern. Currently blue is both less popular and less abundant. Pieces in green have been reported as well, but these are quite scarce.

A wide variety of items were produced in the pattern, including a Thanksgiving set with turkey platter and oversized "buffet" plates. The following table displays a list of the American scenes included in the pattern and the piece on which they are imprinted.

Scene	Item
Home for Thanksgiving	Turkey Platter
Frozen Up	Buffet Plate
Richmond, Virginia	Round Vegetable Bowl
Capitol at Williamsburg	Cream Soup and Liner
San Francisco	Teacup and Saucer
R.R. Valley of the Mohawk	Creamer
The Clermont	Covered Sugar Bowl

The Flying Cloud	Chop Plate
Low Water in the Mississippi	Sauce Boat
Wall Street	Luncheon Plate
Broadway	Small (12") Platter
Michigan Avenue, Chicago	Rim Soup
Central Park, Grand Drive	Coffee Mug
Brooklyn Ferry	Cream Soup Bowl
New York Crystal Palace	Handled Cake Plate
The Rocky Mountains	Bread and Butter
The Mail and the Stage Coach	Ashtray
Natural Bridge of Virginia	Fruit Bowl
Niagara Falls	Small (11½") Platter
The White House	Demitasse Cup
The Capitol at Washington	Square Salad Plate
Mount Vernon	Teapot
Monticello	Milk Pitcher
Hancock House	Cereal Bowl
Independence Hall	Large (16") Platter
Boston, Massachusetts	Dinner Plate
Sacramento City, California	Sandwich Plate
The Alamo	Coffee Cup
New Orleans, Louisiana	Relish Dish or Sauceboat Liner
Fort Dearborn	Double Egg Cup
Washington, D.C.	Medium (14") Platter
West Point	Coupe Soup
Kansas City, Missouri	Covered Vegetable Bowl
The Erie Canal	Oval Vegetable Bowl

Historic America brown square salad plate $18-20, dinner plate $30-35, lunch plate $22-25, bread and butter plate $10-12, cup/saucer $18-20, fruit $10-12.

Historic America brown covered sugar $45-50, creamer $40-45, milk pitcher $90-100.

Historic America brown turkey platter $225-250.

Historic America brown 16" large platter $150-175, 10" small platter $65-75.

Historic America brown rim soup $18-20

Historic America brown buffet plate $35-40, dinner plate $30-35.

Historic America pink sauceboat $40-45, relish/sauceboat liner $30-35, small platter $75-85, medium platter $110-120, covered sugar $50-55, oval vegetable $60-65.

Historic America pink demitasse cup/saucer $35-40, handled cake plate $120-130, jumbo
cup $35-40, coffee cup and saucer $20-22, teacup/saucer $18-20.

Historic America pink buffet plate $60-70.

Historic America pink medium pitcher $100-110.

Historic America backstamp.

Historic America ashtrays. Pink $30-35, blue $30-35.

Historic America blue ashtray $30-35, teapot $150-175.

Historic America blue chop plate $100-110, relish/ underliner $30-35.

Item	Blue	Pink	Brown
Ashtray	$30-35	$30-35	$30-35
Bowl, creamsoup w/liner	$30-35	$35-40	$35-40
Bowl, fruit	$6-7	$12-15	$10-12
Bowl, fruit tab	$12-15	$15-18	$15-128
Bowl, cereal	$8-10	$15-18	$15-18
Bowl, tab cereal	$15-18	$18-20	$18-20
Bowl, rim soup	$15-18	$18-20	$18-20
Bowl. 8 1/2" round vegetable	$35-40	$55-60	$45-50
Bowl, 9 1/2" round vegetable	$40-45	$60-65	$50-60
Bowl, oval vegetable, 2 sizes	$40-45	$60-65	$50-60
Bowl, covered vegetable	$120-130	$160-175	$150-160
Coaster	$12-15	$18-20	$18-20
Coffeepot	$150-175	$175-195	$175-195
Creamer	$30-35	$40-45	$40-45
Cup/saucer, tea	$15-18	$18-20	$18-20
Cup/saucer, coffee	$18-20	$20-22	$18-20
Cup/saucer demitasse	$22-25	$35-40	$30-35
Cup/saucer, jumbo	$30-35	$40-45	$40-45
Cup/saucer joke large	$125-150	$150-175	$150-175
Eggcup, double	$30-35	$35-40	$30-35
Mug	$18-20	$24-26	$24-26
Pitcher, milk small	$60-70	$90-100	$80-90
Pitcher, medium	$75-85	$100-110	$90-100
Plate, bread and butter	$6-7	$10-12	$10-12
Plate, round salad	$12-14	$18-20	$18-20
Plate, square salad	$18-20	$18-20	$18-20
Plate, lunch	$18-20	$22-25	$22-25
Plate, dinner	$18-20	$30-35	$30-35
Plate snack w/ cup	$22-25	$25-30	$25-30
Plate, buffet	$22-25	$60-70	$35-40
Plate, handled cake	$90-100	$120-130	$100-110
Plate, lg. Chop	$100-110	$120-130	$120-130
Platter 10"	$45-50	$75-85	$65-75
Platter 12"	$50-60	$110-120	$90-100
Platter 14"	$75-85	$120-130	$100-110
Platter 16"	$120-130	$150-175	$150-175
Platter, 20" Turkey	$200-225	$325-350	$225-250
Relish/liner	$30-35	$30-35	$30-35
Sauceboat	$40-45	$40-45	$40-45
Sauceboat, fast-stand	$75-85	$85-95	$85-95
Sugar, covered	$40-45	$50-55	$45-50
Teapot	$150-175	$225-250	$200-225
Tureen, covered	$350-400	$400-450	$375-425

Italian (Spode's Italian) – Spode

One of the most classic and enduring English transferware patterns is Spode's Italian, which has been in continuous production since its introduction in 1816. The pattern integrates an 18th century Chinese border treatment with a central scene based upon an original 17th century engraving housed at the Spode factory. The scene is believed to depict ruins near Rome, with figures of people and animals fancifully integrated into the foreground.

Spode's Italian has been primarily produced in a bright, vivid shade of blue called "Ultramarine Blue" on earthenware blanks. In addition, a line of giftware was produced for Tiffany and Company with the Italian pattern printed in black with gold trim. Rarely encountered are pieces of Spode's Italian in mulberry or plum, and a vintage butterpat in pink was quite a surprising discovery. The Italian pattern was also produced on bone china blanks with gold trim on a limited basis.

With such a long period of production, a multitude of marks were employed on Spode's Italian pieces. The earliest Spode's Italian items were produced on a bluish tinted pearlware body. The impressed and/or printed "Spode" and "SPODE" marks are the earliest, dating from 1816 to 1833. At this time, the pattern was widely copied, and pieces can be found with the names of other British potteries. The "Copeland Late Spode" mark was introduced around 1890, and is not frequently encountered. The oval printed mark was used from the 1890s through the 1960s. It was followed by the blue mark and subsequently the black mark. The most recent production marks often include the words "microwave safe."

Spode's Italian, as a pattern, is a collector's dream. Hundreds and hundreds of pieces have been produced in the pattern over the past 180 years, with virtually every unusual and even exotic serving piece imaginable awaiting discovery by the serious collector. In addition to dinnerware, complete wash sets were produced, along with matching vanity sets with a variety of covered jars and containers for milady's potions. It seems just about every imaginable piece has been made in Spode's Italian – from garden planters and stools to even bathroom sinks!

Italian creamsoup with liner $35-40, fruit bowl $15-18, cereal $18-20, small rim soup $20-25, large rim soup $30-35, dinner plate $30-35, lunch plate $25-30, bread and butter plate $12-15, teacup and saucer $20-25, coffee cup and saucer $22-25.

Italian novelty jumbo cup/saucer (with Auld Lang Syne) $50-60, jumbo cup and saucer $40-45.

Italian cereal bowl variants.

Italian rim soup variants.

Italian round serving tray $90-100

Italian children's pieces. Creamer, sugar, plate, cup/saucer $50-60 each.

Italian crescent salads. Small 30-35, large $40-45.

Italian bowls: round vegetable $40-45, small deep round vegetable $65-75, large salad $120-130.

54

Italian early pearlware dinner plate $75-85, platter $350-400, rim soup $50-60.

Italian square sandwich plates $20-25 each, rectangular sandwich tray $130-150.

Italian square luncheon plate $35-40, square sandwich plate $20-25.

Italian octagonal divided sandwich plate $35-40, octagonal cake plate $90-100, handled cake plate $125-150.

Italian small platter $75-85, extra large platter $225-275, medium platter $120-130, large platter $175-195, small platter $85-95

Italian turkey platter $350-400.

Italian divided vegetable $300-325, small vegetable $65-75, handled vegetable $100-125, rimmed square vegetable $75-85.

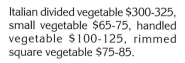

Italian sauce tureen liners: Oval
Pearlware $125-150, round $75-85.

Italian diamond-shaped
relish $50-60.

Italian pearlware "tree and well"
platter $650-750.

Italian pearlware meat drain $200-225.

Italian creamer $40-45, waste bowl $60-70, open sugar $45-50.

Italian novelty teapots: Left $175-195, middle $150-175, right $200-225.

Italian large water kettle $500-550, teacup/saucer $20-25.

Italian graduated teapots. Small $100-125, medium $150-175, large $175-195, medium $145-165.

Italian small hot water pot $85-95, large hot water pot $125-150, small coffeepot $150-175, large coffeepot $175-200.

Italian graduated Dutch jugs $75-90 each.

Italian small octagonal pitcher $125-145, large octagonal pitcher $165-185.

Italian demitasse coffeepot $175-200, demitasse cup/saucer $35-40.

Italian Canterbury or supper set with mahogany lazy susan $1300-1500.

Italian wash bowls and pitchers. Regular $450-500, individual $300-350.

Italian sauce tureen with liner $225-275, large c. 1820 pearlware soup tureen $1200-1500, large soup tureen with liner $550-650.

Italian large cheese wedge $150-175, small cheese box $200-225.

Italian biscuit barrel with reed handle $200-225, biscuit jar $200-225.

Italian oil jar/vase $125-150, covered wine carafe $600-650.

Italian divided relish trays. 5-part leaf $300-350, 3-part diamond $150-175, 6-part round chip and dip $275-300, 3-part handled $160-175.

Italian banana stand $300-325, 12" footed cake stand $225-250.

Italian "Who burnt the table cloth" ashtray $30-35, handled porringer $100-125, leaf bonbon $65-75.

Italian (from left) individual mint jelly $35-40, individual sauce boat liner $40-45, round butter pat $22-25 octagonal butter pat $25-30, seashell salt dish $25-30.

Italian ramekin and saucer $50-60,
covered onion soup $65-75.

Italian Temple jars $125-150 each.

Italian spill vases $75-85 each, large
octagonal vase $125-150.

Italian tumbler $30-40, toothbrush
holder $40-45, pomade jar $85-95.

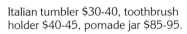

Italian eggcups $30-35 each, eggcup tray $100-125.

Italian eggcups $30-35 each.

Italian 3-handled "tyg" mug $200-225, mug $30-35, hot chocolate cup/saucer $50-60.

Italian pepper shaker $35-40, tea tile $85-95, toast rack $175-200, eggcup $30-35.

Italian footed hot plate/tea tile $125-150, small toast rack $90-100, covered vegetable $160-175.

Italian bone china gold-trimmed cup/saucer $18-20.

Italian go-along biscuit tin $30-35.

Italian black individual
ashtray/coaster $18-20.

Italian pink butter pat $25-30. Custom-
made for Philadelphia socialite.

Italian lavender teapot $175-200, cup/saucer $20-25.

Italian old backstamps

Italian new backstamp.

Liberty Blue – Royal Staffordshire

As America prepared to celebrate its Bicentennial, a popular line of English transferware was introduced. In 1975, Liberty Blue was marketed as a promotional line for the Benjamin Franklin Federal Savings and Loan in the Pacific Northwest as well as for a number of grocery store chains across the nation.

With a simple bank deposit or grocery purchase, Liberty Blue dinner plates, bread and butter plates, fruit bowls, and cups and saucers were available for purchase at deeply discounted, bargain prices. Additional place setting pieces and serving pieces were available for purchase at reasonable retail prices for those customers wishing to complete their sets. For this reason, these basic place setting pieces are still readily available on the secondary market and remain at "bargain prices" compared to items in other collectible English transferware patterns, while other place setting pieces and serving pieces command comparable prices to those in other discontinued collectible dinnerware patterns.

Liberty Blue's border treatment is an adaptation from an early 19th century historical Staffordshire border containing wild flowers. A total of fifteen different historical American scenes appear across the place setting and serving pieces made for the pattern. The available pieces and the scenes they depict are presented in the pricing table for this pattern.

Liberty Blue fruit $5-7, dinner $6-8, bread and butter $4-6, cup/saucer $4-6.

Liberty Blue mug $15-18, medium platter $50-55, salad plate $12-14, flat soup $22-25, cereal bowl $12-15.

Liberty Blue covered vegetable $100-125, large platter $75-85, round vegetable $35-40.

Liberty Blue original box for covered vegetable.

Liberty Blue sauceboat $35-40, soup tureen $325-375, milk pitcher $125-150, covered butter dish $45-50, creamer $20-25, covered sugar $30-35.

Liberty Blue, 3 of the 4 coasters $12-15 each.

Liberty Blue salt and pepper $25-30, lunch plate $25-30, teapot $125-150, sauceboat $35-40, liner $20-25

Liberty Blue go-along large turkey platter $100-125.

Liberty Blue backstamp.

Item	Scene	Blue
Bowl, fruit	Betsy Ross	$5-7
Bowl, cereal	Mount Vernon	$12-15
Bowl, soup rim	Old North Church	$22-25
Bowl, oval vegetable	Minute Men	$40-50
Bowl, round vegetable	Faunces Tavern	$34-40
Bowl, covered vegetable	Boston Tea Party	$100-125
Butter dish	Lafayette Landing at West Point	$45-50
Coasters (4 scenes)	Faunces Tavern, Paul Revere, Independence Hall, Old North Chruch	$10-12
Creamer	Paul Revere	$20-25
Cup/saucer	Paul Revere/Old North Church	$4-6
Mug	Monticello	$15-18
Pitcher, milk	Old North Church	$125-150
Placecards	Eagle	$20-25
Plate, 6" B&B	Monticello	$4-6
Plate 7" salad	Washington Leaving Christ Church	$12-14
Plate, 9" lunch	Washington at Valley Forge	$25-30
Plate 10" dinner	Independence Hall	$6-8
Platter, medium	Governor's House Williamsburg	$50-55
Platter, large	Washington Crossing the Delaware	$75-85
Platter, turkey go-along	Declaration of Independence Scene	$100-125
Relish/Liner	Governor's House Williamsburg	$20-25
Salt and Pepper	Paul Revere	$25-30
Sauceboat	Lafayette Landing at West Point	$35-40
Sugar	Betsy Ross	$30-35
Teapot	Minute Men	$150-175
Tureen	Boston Tea Party/Minute Men	$325-375

Old Britain Castles – Johnson Brothers

Old Britain Castles has been produced by Johnson Brothers from the early 1930s to the present, and is a widely recognized and popular pattern. It is most readily available in pink, but was also produced in blue, brown multicolored, lavender and green. Lavender Old Britain Castles is quite scarce, with most pieces bearing only the earliest "Old Britain Castles, England, Johnson Brothers," backstamp. Green Old Britain Castles seems to have been marketed almost exclusively to continental Europe.

As alluded to above, Old Britain Castles pieces can be "dated" by their varying backstamps. The first backstamp bearing only "Old Britain Castles, England, Johnson Brothers," dates from the 1930s into the 1940s. With the advent of harsher detergents in the late 1940s, the phrases, "all decoration under the glaze" and "permanent and acid resisting colors" were added to the backstamp. The words "Dishwasher Safe" were introduced in the 1960s. In 1970, "Royal Warrants" backstamps were introduced having the wording "by appointment to her majesty the queen manufacturers of ceramic tablewares." Backstamps from the 1980s and 1990s include the words, "Microwave Safe."

Being an "earlier," 1930s pattern, a wide variety of both place setting and serving pieces are available. Years ago the author owned a fish serving platter in Old Britain Castles. It included four different castle transfers in its design. The platter sold to the first collector I showed it to – so quickly I did not have the chance to note which four castles it depicted!

Following is a partial list of items and the castles they depict.

Item	Castle(s) Depicted
Dinner Plate	Blarney Castle
Salad Plate (Square)	Belvoir Castle
Fruit Bowl	Alnwick Castle
Cereal Bowl (Square)	City of Exeter
Teacup	Stratford-on-Avon and Penshurst, Kent
Oval Vegetable Bowl	Ragland Castle
Small Platter	Cambridge
Creamer	Goodrich Castle and Brougham Castle
Sugar Bowl	Kirkstall Abbey and Powderham Castle

Old Britain Castles pink rim soup $18-20, salad plate $12-15, dinner plate $18-20, mug $20-25, cup/saucer $10-12, creamsoup/liner $30-35.

Old Britain Castles pink 10" rim vegetable $45-50, 8½" round vegetable $40-45, 10" round vegetable $50-60.

Old Britain Castles chop plate $90-100, small platter $50-60, medium platter $65-75, relish/sauceboat liner $30-35.

Old Britain Castles pink covered sugar $35-40, creamer $25-30, small coffeepot $150-175, small teapot $150-175.

Old Britain Castles milk jug $75-85, demitasse creamer $30-35, hot chocolate pot $190-220.

Old Britain Castles lavender tab-handled ice cream $18-20, square salad plate $30-35, dinner plate $30-35, fruit dish $15-18, unusual 2 scene tab bowl $20-25.

Old Britain Castles lavender hot water pot $150-175, demitasse cup/saucer $35-40.

Old Britain Castles lavender soup tureen with picture inside $550-650.

Old Britain Castles inside of soup tureen. Most soup tureens do not have this interior scene.

Old Britain Castles blue large coffeepot $100-110, sauceboat $25-30, 10" platter $25-30, single eggcup $20-25.

Old Britain Castles blue salad plate $10-12, rim soup $15-18, 10" rim vegetable $35-40, jumbo cup/saucer $20-25, bread and butter plate $5-6, demitasse cup/saucer $18-20.

Old Britain Castles green 10" platter $50-60, 11" platter $60-70, demitasse sugar open $40-45, demitasse sugar covered $45-50, demitasse creamer $30-35.

Old Britain Castles brown multi-color square salad $22-25, rim soup $18-20.

Old Britain Castles green salad plate $18-20, dinner plate $22-25, rim soup $18-20, 6½" rim cherry bowl $15-18.

Old Britain Castles new square salad.

Old Britain Castles backstamps – arranged earliest to latest.

Item	Pink	Blue	Lavender	Green	Brown-multi
Bowl, creamsoup/liner	$30-35	$25-30	$35-40		$30-35
Bowl, fruit	$6-7	$5-6	$15-18	$8-10	$8-10
Bowl, tab ice cream	$14-16	$14-16	$18-20		$15-18
Bowl, cereal	$8-10	$7-9	$18-20		$15-18
Bowl, rim cherry 6 1/2"	$12-15	$12-15	$25-30	$15-18	$15-18
Bowl, rim soup	$18-20	$15-18	$18-20	$18-20	$18-20
Bowl, round veg 8 1/2"	$40-45	$20-25	$60-70	$50-60	$50-60
Bowl, round veg 9 1/2"	$50-60	$25-30	$70-80	$55-65	
Bowl, oval veg	$40-45	$20-25	$65-75		$50-60
Bowl, vegetable rim	$45-50	$35-40	$65-75		
Bowl, covered veg (2 styles)	$120-130	$65-75	$150-175		$120-130
Bowl, large salad	$130-150	$75-90	$200-225		
Butter dish, round	$75-90	$45-50	$100-125		
Butter pat	$20-25	$18-20	$165-175		$20-25
Coffeepot, small	$150-175	$90-100	$175-200	$165-175	$165-175
Coffeepot, large	$175-200	$100-110	$175-200		
Creamer, regular	$25-30	$15-18	$40-45	$30-35	$30-35
Creamer, demitasse	$30-35	$18-20	$40-45	$30-35	$30-35
Cup/saucer, tea	$10-12	$7-10	$18-20	$18-20	$15-18
Cup/saucer, demitasse	$15-18	$18-20	$40-45	$30-35	$30-35
Cup/saucer, jumbo	$30-35	$20-25	$45-50		
Eggcup, single	$25-30	$20-25	$30-35	$30-35	
Eggcup, double	$30-35	$24-26	$35-40		
Ginger jar	$150-175	$100-125			
Hot chocolate pot	$190-220	$100-125	$225-250		
Hot water pot	$125-150	$100-125	$150-175		
Jug, milk	$75-85	$50-60	$75-85		
Muffin, covered	$120-130	$75-90	$130-150		
Mug	$20-25	$12-15	$25-30		
Plate, bread and butter	$6-7	$5-6	$12-15	$8-10	$8-10
Plate, salad square	$18-20	$12-14	$30-35	$18-20	$22-25
Plate, salad	$12-15	$10-12	$18-20		$18-20
Plate, lunch	$18-20	$15-18	$25-30		$20-25
Plate, dinner	$18-20	$15-18	$30-35	$22-25	$22-25
Plate, grill	$25-30	$25-30			
Plate, cake handled	$130-150	$30-35	$90-100	$90-100	
Plate, chop	$90-100	$60-70	$120-130	$100-110	
Platter, small 10", 12"	$50-60	$25-30	$75-85	$60-70	$60-70
Platter, medium 14"	$65-75	$30-35	$120-130	$90-100	$90-100
Platter, large 16"	$90-100	$40-50	$175-195		$100-125
Platter, extra large 18"	$140-160	$75-85	$225-275		
Platter, turkey 20"	$200-225	$150-175	$350-400		
Relish/liner	$30-35	$20-25	$40-45	$30-35	$30-35
Sauceboat	$40-45	$25-30	$50-60	$45-50	$45-50
Sauceboat, fast-stand	$75-85	$40-45	$75-85		
Sugar	$35-40	$18-20	$50-60	$40-45	$40-45
Sugar, demitasse (2 styles)	$45-50	$20-25	$50-60	$40-45	$45-50
Teapot, small	$150-175	$100-125	$175-200	$160-165	$160-175
Tureen, soup	$425-475	$425-475	$550-650		$425-475

Rose Chintz – Johnson Brothers

Rose Chintz was designed in the early 1930s and was produced using a pink transfer with multicolored tinting. For a brief time in the mid 1990s, the pattern was produced using a blue transfer with multicolored tinting, but the line did not enjoy the same popularity as the original pink with multicolored version of the pattern.

As with Old Britain Castles, Rose Chintz pieces can be dated by their varying backstamps. The first backstamp bearing only "Rose Chintz, England, Johnson Brothers," dates from the 1930s into the 1940s. With the advent of harsher detergents in the late 1940s, the phrases, "all decoration under the glaze" and "permanent and acid resisting colors" were added to the backstamp. The words "Dishwasher Safe" were introduced in the 1960s. In 1970, "Royal Warrants" backstamps were introduced including the wording "by appointment to her majesty the queen manufacturers of ceramic tablewares." Backstamps from the 1980s and 1990s include the words, "Microwave Safe."

A wide variety of place setting and serving pieces can be found in Rose Chintz. When displayed together, the demitasse creamer, regular creamer, small Dutch jug (milk), and large Dutch jug (water) form a lovely graduated pitcher set.

Rose Chintz rim soup $15-18, square salad plate $18-20, dinner plate $18-20, bread and butter plate $5-7, luncheon plate $18-20, double eggcup $30-35, cup/saucer $15-18, fruit bowl $5-7, cereal bowl $10-12, tab cereal $14-16.

Rose Chintz oval vegetable $40-45, medium platter $65-75,
small round vegetable $30-35.

Rose Chintz medium Dutch jug $60-70, large Dutch jug $65-75, covered coffeepot $140-
160, regular creamer $28-30, demitasse creamer $30-35.

Rose Chintz demitasse sugar $40-45, demitasse creamer $30-35.

Rose Chintz 12½" chop plate $100-110.

Rose Chintz backstamps. Left: early coffeepot base. Right: new creamer base with no ink stamp, embossed "Made in England".

A GENUINE HAND ENGRAVING
ROSE CHINTZ
MADE IN ENGLAND
BY
Johnson Bros
ALL DECORATION UNDER
THE GLAZE PERMANENT &
ACID RESISTING COLOR
PAT. NO. 160,783

Rose Chintz backstamps arranged earliest to latest.

Tonquin – Royal Staffordshire, Royal Crownford, Alfred Meakin

Tonquin is a 1940s Royal Staffordshire translation of a 19th century design by world famous English ceramicist Clarice Cliff. The design has a floral border with trim containing beads and flowers. The center scene is a romanticized oriental landscape with surreal floral components framing the scene.

The Tonquin pattern can be found on an amazing number of items ranging from dinnerware to kitchen accessories to lamps and other decorative items. The main place setting pieces and serving pieces were produced in five main colorways: pink, purple, blue, brown, and brown with multicolored tinting. Novelty items, such as vases, and unusual place setting pieces, such as bone dishes and individual sorbet comports, were also produced in black and green. We continue to "discover" new pieces on a regular basis, and welcome our readers to write us about additional items they encounter.

Our research suggests that Royal Staffordshire and Royal Crownford Tonquin items were produced from the 1940s into the 1960s, followed by Alfred Meakin production of the pattern in the 1970s. Myott items produced on swirled blanks seem to be the most recent issue of the Tonquin pattern, and as such, command much lower prices.

Tonquin (Clarice Cliff) pink mug $20-25, bread and butter plate $10-12, salad plate $18-20, dinner plate $30-35, cup/saucer $18-20, rim soup $18-20.

Tonquin (Clarice Cliff) pink barrel shaker $60-70, teapot $275-300, utility tray $22-25, covered sugar $50-60.

Tonquin (Clarice Cliff) pink toast rack $100-110, biscuit cradle $90-100, 8" round vegetable $50-60, small square ashtray $22-25.

Tonquin (Myott) pink scalloped soup bowl $10-12.

Tonquin (Royal Crownford) pink tea tile $75-85.

Tonquin (Clarice Cliff) pink 3-tier tidbit $75-85.

Tonquin (Clarice Cliff) pink individual sorbet/master salt $50-60, urn vase $50-60, jack-in-the-pulpit vase $90-100, chamber stick $60-70.

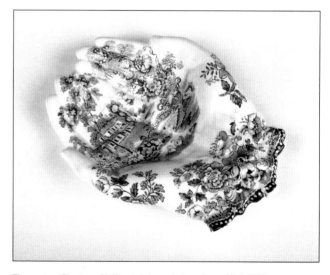

Tonquin (Clarice Cliff) pink hands bonbon $90-100.

Tonquin (Clarice Cliff) pink 9½" candlesticks $250-275 pair.

Tonquin (Clarice Cliff) pink handled candlesticks $90-100 each.

Tonquin (Clarice Cliff) blue bread and butter plate $6-8, salad plate $15-18, dinner plate $18-20, cup/saucer $15-18.

Tonquin (Clarice Cliff) blue fruit $5-7, rim soup $18-20.

Tonquin (Clarice Cliff) blue 8" round vegetable $35-40, 9" round vegetable $40-45.

Tonquin (Clarice Cliff) blue handled tray $60-70, 11" platter $50-55.

Tonquin (Clarice Cliff) blue round ashtray $18-20, individual creamer $18-20, toast tray $90-100.

Tonquin (Clarice Cliff) blue Dutch jug $50-60, covered sugar $30-35, barrel shaker $30-35 each.

Tonquin (Clarice Cliff) blue teapot $160-175, butter dish $60-70, urn vase $45-50.

Tonquin (Myott) blue dinner plate $10-12.

Tonquin (Clarice Cliff) blue sorbet/master salt $45-50, round tea tile $60-70, shoe planter $45-50.

Tonquin (Clarice Cliff) blue square salad plate $60-70, 9" round lunch plate $45-50, rim soup $15-18.

Tonquin (Clarice Cliff) purple rim soup $18-20, dinner plate $30-35, salad plate $18-20, bread and butter plate $12-15, cup/saucer $18-20.

Tonquin (Clarice Cliff) purple round vegetable $65-75, platter $125-135, salad bowl $90-100.

Tonquin (Clarice Cliff) brown rim soup $18-20, dinner plate $25-30, salad plate $15-18, bread and butter plate $8-10, coffee mug $20-25, double eggcup $35-40, cup/saucer $18-20.

Tonquin (Clarice Cliff) brown round vegetable $50-60, platter $75-85, round cigar ashtray $30-35.

Tonquin (Clarice Cliff) brown soup tureen with liner and ladle $450-500.

Tonquin (Clarice Cliff) brown soup tureen liner $100-125..

Tonquin (Clarice Cliff) brown toast holder $90-100, coaster $22-25, shoe $50-60.

Tonquin (Clarice Cliff) brown (center) tankard pitcher $70-80, individual creamers (2 styles) $24-26, demitasse creamer $35-40, demitasse sugar $40-45, small creamer (Meakin) $25-30.

Tonquin (Clarice Cliff) brown regular salt and pepper $45-50 pair, urn vase $50-60, cigarette box $100-110, covered butter dish $75-90.

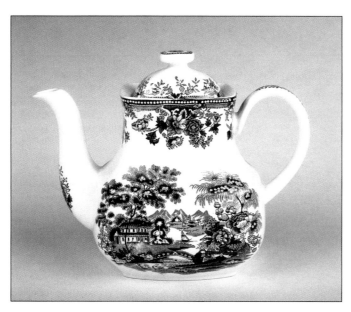

Tonquin (Meakin) brown teapot $100-110

Tonquin (Clarice Cliff) brown biscuit jar $225-275.

Tonquin (Clarice Cliff) brown 8 1/2" wall pocket vase $175-200.

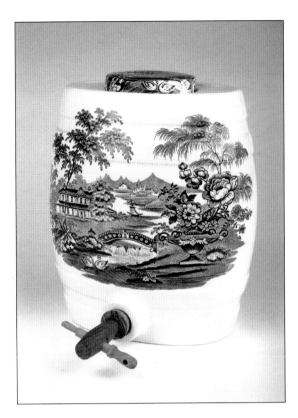

Tonquin (Royal Crownford) brown 12" x 10" water cooler $250-300.

Close-up of water cooler cover.

Tonquin (Meakin) brown demitasse cup/saucer $20-25.

Tonquin (Clarice Cliff) green individual sauceboat and liner $30-35.

Tonquin (Clarice Cliff) green sorbet/master salt $50-60.

Tonquin (Clarice Cliff) black planter $45-60, individual sauceboat and liner $30-35.

Tonquin (Clarice Cliff) brown multi-color salad plate $18-20, bread and butter plate $10-12, dinner plate $30-35, cup/saucer $15-18, fruit $12-15.

Tonquin (Meakin) brown multi-color cereal $8-10, large platter $100-110, small platter $50-60.

Tonquin (Clarice Cliff) brown multi-color large oval vegetable $70-80, medium oval vegetable $60-70.

Tonquin (Clarice Cliff) brown multi-color creamer $40-45, covered sugar $50-60

Tonquin (Clarice Cliff) crescent salads $14-16 each.

Tonquin (Clarice Cliff) ashtrays: blue cigar $30-35, pink cigar $35-40, blue with center cigarette rest $40-45.

Tonquin (Clarice Cliff) blue sorbet/master salt $45-50, black sorbet $50-60, brown demitasse cup/saucer $30-35.

Tonquin (Clarice Cliff) brown multi-color turkey dinner plate $50-60.

Tonquin. Clarice Cliff backstamp.

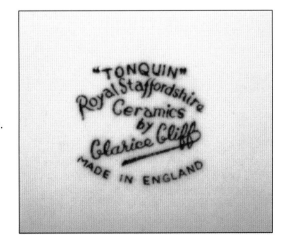

Tower (Spode's Tower) – Spode

Another classic pattern in continuous production for nearly 200 years is Spode's Tower. The design was introduced 1814 and is based upon Merigot's "Bridge of Salaro near Rome" from "Views and Ruins in Rome and its Vicinity" published in 1797-1798. Its central scene is surrounded by a floral border that Spode also used on its "Milkmaid" pattern.

Early Tower pieces were printed in a medium blue, but from the mid-1800s on, a darker blue was used. Late 1800s pieces were often made in "flow blue," where the pigment appears to run or flow under the glaze, rendering the design rather dark and hazy. These flow blue pieces are especially sought after by collectors. In addition to blue, Tower is extremely popular when transfer printed in pink.

On rare occasions, one may find Tower printed in a chocolate brown color, or in chocolate brown with hand tinting.

In both pink and blue, hundreds of pieces have been manufactured over the years, from formal dinnerware, to boudoir and even medical supplies. Sometime between 1890 and 1910, Spode introduced a Tower Thanksgiving or turkey set, comprised of a 17½" platter and 9" plates with a regal tom turkey center. The turkey design was reissued on a larger platter and full-sized dinner plates in the 1940s as part of a game set consisting of the turkey platter, and 12 numbered plates each featuring a different game bird center. These turkey pieces have become especially prized by both collectors of Spode's Tower and collectors of turkey china in general.

Tower pink dinner plate $30-35, lunch plate $25-28, toddy/bread and butter plate $15-20, salad plate $18-20, small rim soup $20-25, demitasse cup/saucer $35-40, cup/saucer $20-25.

Tower pink 8½" square luncheon plate $75-85.

Tower pink (front) 10½" rectangular vegetable $90-100, (back) 9" rectangular vegetable $75-80, 8" square vegetable $75-85.

Tower pink dresser tray $160-175, covered sugar $50-60, creamer $40-45, teapot $175-200.

Tower large soup tureen liner $175-200.

Tower pink small soup tureen $425-475.

Tower pink scalloped oval vegetable bowl $140-160, octagonal vegetable $185-215.

Tower pink 13" platter $110-120, 17" platter $225-275, 14½" platter $150-175.

Tower pink 3-part center handled relish $175-200, 9¾" tazza/ compote $200-225.

Tower pink covered muffin $130-150, covered vegetable $160-175.

Tower pink fast-stand sauceboat $90-100, round tea tile $125-150, milk jug $175-200.

Tower pink banana stand $300-325.

Tower pink 6½" candlesticks $350-400 pair.

Tower pink 15" chop plate $175-195.

Tower pink butter pat $20-25.

Tower go-along tin $20-30.

Tower blue large rim soup $30-35, salad plate $20-22, bread and butter plate $12-15, lunch plate $25-30, dinner plate $30-35, creamsoup with liner $40-45, cup/saucer $20-25.

Tower blue butter pat $22-25, double eggcup $35-40, single eggcup $30-35.

Tower blue jumbo cup/saucer $45-50, teacup/saucer $20-25, demitasse cup/saucer $45-50.

Tower blue tazza $200-225.

Tower blue different styles of after dinner saucers. Left: scarce $20-25; right $8-10.

Tower blue square salad bowl $100-110, early scalloped salad bowl $200-225.

Tower blue large scalloped tray $200-225, small scalloped tray $175-200.

Tower blue waste bowl $60-70, demitasse coffeepot $175-200, coffeepot $150-175, high-handled milk pitcher $100-110, high-handled creamer $75-90, Dutch jug $75-85.

Tower blue 4-slice toast holder $130-150, round covered cheese/butter $160-175.

Tower blue 13" rectangular sandwich tray $130-150, 11½" chop plate $120-130, 9¾" platter $75-85.

Tower blue mayo rope edge $100-110, mayo no rope $100-110, covered mustard $120-130.

Tower blue large scalloped strawberry bowl $140-160, small scalloped strawberry bowl $130-150.

Tower salad plates: flow blue $30-35, oval backstamp $18-20, new backstamp NV.

Tower Turkey plate $200-225.

Tower backstamps – arranged
earliest to latest.

Spode's Tower catalogue pages, ca. 1950.

TOWER (Blue or Pink)

Gadroon Shape

Priced from September, 1959 Retail Price Scale H-15

Additional items ordered from Complete Retail Price Scale will be delivered in
1 - 2 months

Plates 10" (Dinner)	33.60 dz. - 2.80 ea.
Plates 8¼" (Breakfast or Luncheon)	31.20 dz. - 2.60 ea.
Plates 7" (Tea or Salad)	25.20 dz. - 2.10 ea.
Crescent Salad Plates (Large Size)	42.00 dz. - 3.50 ea.
Plates 6" (Large Bread & Butter)	21.60 dz. - 1.80 ea.
Plates 5" (Small Bread & Butter)	21.60 dz. - 1.80 ea.
Individual Ash Trays (Butters)	12.00 dz. - 1.00 ea.
Rim Soups 8"	32.40 dz. - 2.70 ea.
Rim Soups 7"	25.20 dz. - 2.10 ea.
Oatmeals 6" (Cereal Dish)	27.60 dz. - 2.30 ea.
Fruit Saucers 5"	20.40 dz. - 1.70 ea.
Square Dessert Plates	33.60 dz. - 2.80 ea.
Tea Cups & Saucers	37.20 dz. - 3.10 ea.
After Dinner Cups & Saucers	33.60 dz. - 2.80 ea.
Irish Cups & Saucers (Large Cup)	47.40 dz. - 3.95 ea.
Cream Soup Bowls & Stands	56.40 dz. - 4.70 ea.
Double Egg Cups	36.00 dz. - 3.00 ea.
Square Cake Plate	8.30 ea.
Dish 10" (Platter)	7.60 ea.
Dish 12" (Platter)	10.50 ea.
Dish 14" (Platter)	14.50 ea.
Dish 16" (Platter)	20.00 ea.
Dish 18" (Platter)	29.50 ea.
Dish 22" (Platter)	49.50 ea.
Round Chop 12" (Round Platter)	13.00 ea.
Round Chop 14" (Round Platter)	20.00 ea.
Baker 8" (Open Vegetable Dish)	7.70 ea.
Baker 9" (Open Vegetable Dish)	8.40 ea.
Baker 10" (Open Vegetable Dish)	9.10 ea.
Baker, Divided 12" (Open Vegetable Dish)	15.50 ea.
Divided Vegetable Dish 10"	11.30 ea.
Square Scallop 8" (Open Fruit or Salad Bowl)	8.40 ea.
Square Scallop 9" (Open Fruit or Salad Bowl)	9.10 ea.
Covered Dish 10" (Vegetable Dish)	22.50 ea.
Sauce Boat (Gravy) Stand attached	14.00 ea.
Covered Sauce Tureen & Stand (1 Pint)	18.50 ea.
Covered Soup Tureen & Stand 11" (4 Quarts)	55.00 ea.
Round Salad Bowl 10" Footed	22.50 ea.
§Pickle Dish	5.60 ea.
*Bowl 30's (Bowl 5½")	3.30 ea.
Bowl 36's (Bowl 5")	2.70 ea.
Teapot (8 Cups) (Regular)	13.50 ea.
Teapot (Individual Size)	10.50 ea.
Covered Sugar (Regular)	9.10 ea.
Covered Sugar (Individual Size)	8.40 ea.

Cream (Regular)	5.40 ea.
Cream (Individual Size)	4.40 ea.
Coffee Pot 12's (12 Cups)	17.00 ea.
Coffee Pot 18's (8 Cups)	15.00 ea.
Coffee Pot 36's (Individual Size)	10.50 ea.
Jug 12's, Low Dutch (2½ Pints)	9.80 ea.
Jug 24's, Low Dutch (1½ Pints)	6.30 ea.
Jug 36's, Low Dutch (¾ Pint)	4.40 ea.
Jug 18's, Tall Gadroon (2½ Pints)	7.50 ea.
Jug 24's, Tall Gadroon (2¼ Pints)	6.30 ea.
Jug 30's, Tall Gadroon (1½ Pints)	5.40 ea.
Jug 36's, Tall Gadroon (1 Pint)	4.40 ea.
Covered Jug 36's (¾ Pint)	6.50 ea.
Round Punch Bowl 15" Footed	78.50 ea.
Tea Kettle (Large) (4 Quarts)	34.00 ea.
Tea Kettle (Small) (2 Quarts)	29.50 ea.
Covered Butter Dish (½ Pound)	7.00 ea.
Covered Canterbury Set	126.00 ea.
Wood Tray for Canterbury Set	24.00 ea.
Joke Cup & Saucer	7.70 ea.
Dish 22" (Turkey Platter) (Turkey Center)	55.00 ea.
Plates 10" (Game Centers)	38.40 dz. - 3.20 ea.
Salt & Pepper Shaker Set (2 pieces)	7.00 ea.
§Jubilee Tray	8.40 ea.
Cake Stand	16.00 ea.
§Pepper Mill	10.00 ea.
Tier Tray	13.70 ea.

EXTRA SERVING PIECES

Comport (Low) 3" high—10" diameter	10.50 ea.
Relish Dish (Ameer) 15½" long—4" wide	10.80 ea.
Berry Dish 9" (Oval)	11.10 ea.
Berry Dish 8" (Oval)	8.90 ea.
Berry Dish 7" (Oval)	8.00 ea.
Berry Dish 6" (Oval)	6.60 ea.
Roll Tray	16.00 ea.
Severn Sweet (Ring Handled Relish Dish)	5.80 ea.
Twin Sweet (Ring Handled Relish Dish)	11.20 ea.
Chelsea Shell 6"	7.70 ea.
§Pink only	

Individual Place Setting (5 Pieces) 9.80

1—Dinner Plate; 1—Tea or Salad Plate; 1—Bread & Butter Plate; 1—Tea Cup; 1—Saucer

*Blue only   §Pink only

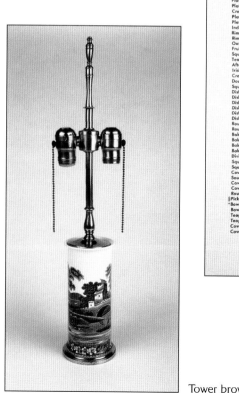

Tower brown lamp $225-275.

Vista – Mason's

Mason's Vista was designed in the early 1800s and is comprised of a wide variety of romanticized landscape scenes united by a grape leaf border. Most pieces are produced on Mason's "Gadroon" shape, inspired by the rope-edged design popular in Georgian sterling silver, but novelty items in the pattern abound, and tableware and "fancy" items are found on other Mason's shapes as illustrated in the 1940s brochure that follows. Vista is most commonly found in blue, pink, and brown. Infrequently pieces of Vista with the transfer printed in purple with hand tinted colors can be found.

For dating Vista pieces, backstamps that do not include "England" are the earliest – from the 19th century. The Mason's Vista England backstamp dates from the first half of the 1900s, while the backstamp indicating "Permanent and Acid Resisting Colors" was introduced shortly after World War II in the late 1940s. Vista has been produced off and on throughout the past two centuries, even as ownership and pattern rights to the Mason's name have changed. Vista's classic beauty and abundance of serving pieces and decorative items makes it exceedingly popular with today's collectors.

Vista pink lunch plate $22-25, bread and butter plate $12-15, salad plate $18-20, dinner plate $30-35, creamsoup/liner $35-40, cup/saucer $18-20.

Vista sales brochure.

Vista pink fast-stand gravy $70-80, square tray $85-95, octagonal bowls $40-45 each, footed compote $175-200.

Vista pink jumbo cup/saucer
$45-50, child's mug $50-60.

Vista pink small round vegetable
bowl $50-60, 12¼" flat cake
plate $180-200, oval vegetable
bowl $50-55, creamer $30-35.

Vista pink footed
serpent bowl $300-
325, Fenton jug
$100-110, cheese
wedge $120-130

Vista pink Hydra pitchers: small $75-85, medium $100-110, large $110-120.

Vista pink fan-shape tea set. Creamer $30-35, tea caddy $75-85, covered sugar bowl $50-60, teapot $175-200.

Vista pink Gadroon tea set. Covered sugar $50-55, creamer $30-35, teapot $150-175.

Vista pink creamer $30-35, covered sugar $50-55, teapot $150-175.

Vista pink large cheese wedge $140-160, small cheese wedge $120-130.

Vista pink cigarette holder $50-60, celery dish $50-60, rectangular sandwich tray $130-150, tri-corn serpent bowl $200-225.

Vista pink large tureen liner $90-100, medium tureen $225-250, ladle $160-170.

Vista pink large Peking salad bowl $300-325.

Vista pink single eggcup $30-35, double eggcup $35-40.

Vista pink butter pat $22-25.

114

Vista pink coupe dinner plate $30-35, coupe salad plate $18-20.

Comparison of regular and coupe dinner plates.

Vista blue turkey plate $50-60, pink $60-70.

Vista blue jumbo cup/saucer $40-45, salad plate $18-20, large round vegetable bowl $60-70, cereal bowl $18-20, large rim soup $30-35.

Vista blue jugs: Fenton $100-110, Hydra $110-120, Gadroon $90-100.

Vista blue sauce tureen ladle $60-70

Vista blue tea tile/hot plate $110-120.

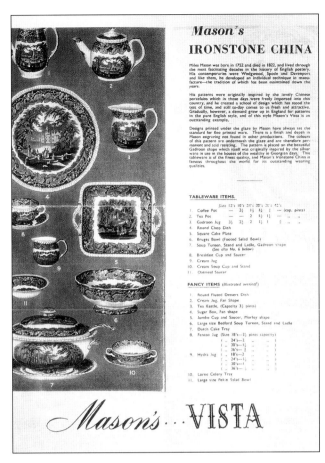

Mason's
IRONSTONE CHINA

Miles Mason was born in 1752 and died in 1822, and lived through the most fascinating decades in the history of English pottery. His contemporaries were Wedgwood, Spode and Davenport and like them, he developed an individual technique in manufacture—the tradition of which has been maintained down the years.

His patterns were originally inspired by the lovely Chinese porcelains which in those days were freely imported into this country, and he created a school of design which has stood the test of time, and still to-day comes to us fresh and attractive. Gradually, however, a demand grew up in England for patterns in the pure English style, and of this style Mason's Vista is an outstanding example.

Designs printed under the glaze by Mason have always set the standard for fine printed ware. There is a finish and depth in Mason engraving not found in other productions. The colours of this pattern are underneath the glaze and are therefore permanent and acid resisting. The pattern is placed on the beautiful Gadroon shape which itself was originally inspired by the silver ware in use in the houses of the wealthy in Georgian days. This tableware is of the finest quality, and Mason's Ironstone China is famous throughout the world for its outstanding wearing qualities.

TABLEWARE ITEMS:

Size 12's 18's 24's 30's 36's 42's 42's

1. Coffee Pot — 2½ 1¾ ½ ¾ (cap. pints)
2. Tea Pot — 3 1½ 1 ¾
3. Gadroon Jug 3½ 2¾ 2 1½ 1 ¾
4. Round Chop Dish
5. Square Cake Plate
6. Bruges Bowl (Footed Salad Bowl)
7. Soup Tureen, Stand and Ladle, Gadroon shape (See also No. 6 below)
8. Breakfast Cup and Saucer
9. Cream Jug
10. Cream Soup Cup and Stand
11. Oatmeal Saucer

FANCY ITEMS (illustrated overleaf)

1. Round Fluted Dessert Dish
2. Cream Jug, Fan Shape
3. Tea Kettle, (Capacity 3½ pints)
4. Sugar Box, Fan shape
5. Jumbo Cup and Saucer, Morley shape
6. Large size Bedford Soup Tureen, Stand and Ladle
7. Dutch Cake Tray
8. Fenton Jug (Size 18's—2½ pints capacity)
   („ 24's—2 „ „)
   („ 30's—1½ „ „)
   („ 36's—1 „ „)
9. Hydra Jug („ 18's—2 „ „)
   („ 24's—1½ „ „)
   („ 30's—1 „ „)
   („ 36's—¾ „ „)
10. Lorne Celery Tray
11. Large size Pekin Salad Bowl

Mason's... VISTA

Vista brochure pages.

Vista brown small Fenton jug $75-85, bread and butter plate $10-12, square vegetable bowl $65-75, double eggcup $35-40, individual ashtray $18-20, fruit bowl $12-15.

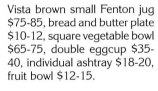

Vista brown large platter $175-200, chowder tureen $250-300, soup tureen ladle $160-175.

117

Vista brown lamp $350-400.

Vista teal ginger jar $50-60.

Vista backstamp – 1940s – 1960s.

Turkey Patterns

Starting in the second half of the 19th century, English potters discovered the American demand for specialized dinnerware for our national feast of Thanksgiving. English potters were all too happy to accommodate the American market with special dinnerware sets depicting cheerful turkey scenes. In some cases, the pottery used the border of a popular existing pattern and simply replaced the center scene to create Thanksgiving pieces. Such patterns as Mason's Vista, Spode's Tower, and Royal Staffordshire's Tonquin were adapted in this way. Other times, potteries created entirely new Thanksgiving patterns, such as Johnson Brothers' His Majesty.

Typically, Thanksgiving sets of the late 1800s included a relatively modest (16"-18") turkey platter and from 6 to 12 relatively small dinner plates – ranging from 9" to 9½". Most often, early turkey sets featured a series of multiple turkey scenes ranging from the solo proud Tom turkey displaying his feathers to his hen and their chicks feeding in the barnyard. During the 20th century, however the turkey platters "grew" to 19" to 24" in length, and plates expanded to the 10" dinner or 10½" buffet plate size. Most 20th century sets depict a single design on all dinner plates and a different design for the platter.

In the past few years, turkey dishes have found a renewed popularity, with some collectors eagerly seeking out pieces in one particular pattern, while others are creating mix and match sets with plates from a variety of patterns and/or manufacturers. Either way, these lovely patterns make a festive holiday table!

Barnyard King (Johnson Bros.) turkey platter $180-200.

Barnyard King (Johnson Bros.) backstamp.

Barnyard King (Johnson Bros.) buffet plate
$45-50, cup/saucer (not shown) $20-25.

His Majesty (Johnson Bros.)
turkey platter $175-200.

His Majesty (Johnson Bros.)
sauceboat and liner $80-100,
buffet plate $40-45, square
salad $40-45, oval vegetable
$90-100, cup/saucer $20-25.

His Majesty (Johnson Bros.) oval vegetable $90-100, with original box add $15-20..

Wild Turkeys Flying (Johnson Bros. – Windsor Ware) buffet plate $50-60

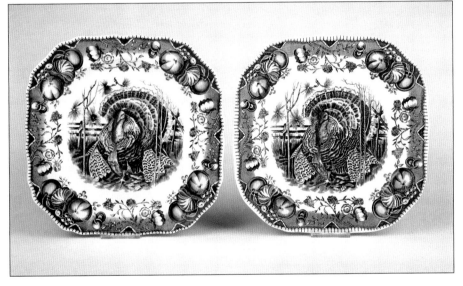

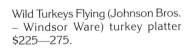

His Majesty (Johnson Bros.) square salad plates. Left: vintage plate. Right: new plate.

Wild Turkeys Flying (Johnson Bros. – Windsor Ware) turkey platter $225—275.

Wild Turkeys (Johnson Bros.)
turkey platter $180-220. (2 sizes)

Wild Turkeys (Johnson Bros.) salad plate
$45-50, buffet plate $40-45, cup/saucer
$20-25, rim soup $45-50.

Wild Turkeys (Johnson Bros.) fast-stand
gravy $100-125, oval vegetable $100-125.

Woodland Wild Turkeys (Johnson Bros.)
brown turkey platter $275-325, green (not
pictured) $250-300.

Woodland Wild Turkeys (Johnson Bros.) green buffet plate $60-70, brown (not shown) $70-80.

Game Birds (Johnson Bros.) – pheasant salad plate $18-20.

Game Birds (Johnson Bros.) –wild turkey dinner plate $25-$30

Game Birds (Johnson Bros.) – quail dinner plate $20-25.

Game Birds (Johnson Bros.) – partridge dinner plate $20-25.

Game Birds (Johnson Bros.) – ruffed grouse dinner plate $20-25.

Game Birds (Johnson Bros.) salad plate and dinner plate.

Game Birds (Johnson Bros.) – woodcock dinner plate $20-25.

Wild Birds of Heath and Moorland (British Anchor) partridge dinner plate $18-20.

Game Birds (Johnson Bros.) coasters. Left: cream background $15-18. Right: white background. $10-12 each.

Wild Birds of Heath and Moorland (British Anchor) golden plover $18-20.

Wood's English Scenery brown multi-color turkey platter $200-250.

Wood's English Scenery pink turkey platter $225-275, blue (not shown) $200-250.

Wood's English Scenery blue multi-color turkey platter $250-300.

Wood's English Scenery brown multi-color dinner plate $50-60. Not shown: blue multi-color $50-60, pink $50-60, blue $45-50.

Wedgwood pink Turkey platter $225-275, turkey dinner plate (not shown) $40-45.

Royal Doulton turkey plate $75-85.
Platter (not shown) $400-450.

Barker Brothers Turkey platter $175-200.

Barker Brothers turkey round vegetable bowl
$60-70, buffet plate $45-50.

Vista blue turkey plate $50-60, pink $60-70.

126

Tonquin (Clarice Cliff) brown multi-color turkey dinner plate $50-60.

Tonquin (Clarice Cliff) brown multi-color turkey platter $200-250.

Spode's Tower blue Game Series 24" platter $1000-1200.

Tower wild duck $175-195.

Tower blackcock $175-195.

Tower woodcock $175-195.

Tower partridge $175-195.

Tower California quail $175-195.

Tower pheasant $175-195.

Tower plover $175-195.

Tower wild geese $175-195.

Tower wild duck $175-195.

Tower grouse $175-195

Tower wood cock $175-195.

Tower turkey $200-225.

Part II: Other Popular Patterns by Company

The second half of this book is dedicated to identifying a wider selection of popular patterns. They are arranged alphabetically by the company that produced them. We have only included a selection of items for each pattern although a wide variety of pieces may have been produced. We recommend referring back to similar patterns in the front section of the book. Many of these pattern were produced on the same or similar blanks as the patterns listed in the front of the book. In some cases, the listing of pieces available and prices for patterns in the front of the book, may be helpful in gathering information on the patterns in the following section.

Booth

British Scenery

British Scenery red lunch plate $15-18, teal dinner plate $18-20, blue bread and butter plate $6-7, teal cup/saucer $12-15, teal double eggcup $25-30, blue creamer $25-30, teal cereal $7-9.

British Scenery blue soup tureen $150-200.

Real Old Willow

Real Old Willow dinner plate $30-35, salad plate $18-20, lunch plate $24-26, bread and butter plate $12-15.

Real Old Willow faststand sauceboat $90-100, teapot $175-195, large soup tureen $550-650.

Booth's Real Old Willow (Royal Doulton). Oval vegetable $40-45, salad plate $12-15, bread and butter plate $8-10, dinner plate $20-25, cup/saucer $15-18.

Real Old Willow single eggcup $35-40.

Real Old Willow backstamps.

Deco. Real Old Willow.

Real Old Willow catalogue page

Crown Ducal

Colonial Times

Colonial Times blue dinner plate $30-35, salad plate $18-20, bread and butter plate $10-12, rim soup $18-20, cup/saucer $20-22, fruit $12-15.

Colonial Times large platter $175-195, creamer $40-45, covered sugar $60-65.

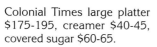

Colonial Times backstamp.

Close-up of sugar finial depicting pilgrim's head. The handles of the sugar bowl have arrows pointing toward the pilgrim's head.

George Washington Bicentenary

George Washington Bicentenary. Washington and Lafayette at Mount Vernon. $30-35

George Washington Bicentenary. Washington's ancestral home. $30-35.

George Washington Bicentenary. Birthplace of Washington at Wakefield, Virginia. $30-35.

Johnson Brothers

Autumn's Delight

Autumn's Delight fruit $5-7, bread and butter plate $5-6, square salad $16-18, dinner plate $12-15, coupe soup $14-16, cup/saucer $8-10.

Autumn's Delight creamer $15-18, covered sugar $22-25, platter $30-35, teapot $80-90, oval vegetable $25-30.

Castle on the Lake

Castle on the Lake blue chop plate $60-70.

Ancient Towers

Ancient Towers. Small coffeepot $90-100, salad plate $10-12.

Castle on the Lake, pink. Oval vegetable $35-40, square salad plate $18-20, dinner plate $18-20, jumbo cup/saucer $30-35.

Chintz

Chintz, lavender. Rim soup $18-20, medium platter $100-110, bread and butter plate $10-12, dinner plate $30-35, covered sugar $45-50, cup/saucer $18-20, fruit bowl $12-15.

Coaching Scenes

Coaching Scenes backstamp.

Coaching Scenes, blue. Round vegetable $20-25, dinner plate $12-15, salad plate $12-15, bread and butter plate $4-6, cereal $10-12.

Dorchester

Dorchester oval vegetable $60-70, extra large platter $225-275, sauceboat $45-50, demitasse creamer $40-45, covered sugar $50-55, waste bowl $60-70.

Dorchester rim soup $18-20, salad plate $20-22, dinner plate $30-35, cup/saucer $18-20.

Dorchester coupe soup $25-30, rim soup $18-20.

Dover

Dover, brown. Rim soup $12-15, bread and butter $3-5, dinner plate $18-20, round vegetable $25-30, creamer $15-18.

Elizabeth

Elizabeth purple oval vegetable $40-45.

Enchanted Garden

Enchanted Garden coffeepot $75-85, square salad plate $12-14, bread and butter plate $5-6.

English Bouquet

English Bouquet (rope edge) sauceboat $50-60, liner $20-25, medium platter $65-75, cup/saucer $18-20, fruit $10-12, bread and butter plate $8-10.

English Bouquet (scalloped) medium platter $65-75, bread and butter plate $8-10, dinner plate $22-25.

137

Exton

Exton, purple round vegetable $30-35, oval vegetable $30-35, platter $40-45, bread and butter plate $4-6, fruit $5-7, cereal $12-15.

Fish

Fish dinner plates $20-25 each.

Fish oval platter $200-225, oval vegetable $50-60.

Garden Bouquet

Garden Bouquet rim soup $15-20, salad plate $10-12, bread and butter plate $5-7, sandwich plate $10-12, lunch plate $12-15, dinner plate $15-18, cup/saucer $10-12, coupe soup $12-15, fruit $6-8.

Garden Bouquet salad plates: square $12-14, round $10-12, "star" $12-14.

Garden Bouquet round vegetable $20-25, creamer $15-18.

Harvest

Harvest turkey platter $225-275. This pattern has the same border as Wild Turkeys Flying and the same center as Windsor Fruit.

Harvest Time

Harvest Time rim soup $15-20, small platter $20-25, dinner plate $15-18, square salad plate $12-14, creamer $15-18, covered sugar $22-25, bread and butter plate $5-6, cup/saucer $10-12.

Harvest buffet plate $50-60, cup/saucer $20-25. Not pictured: Salad plate $50-60, oval vegetable $100-120, fast-stand gravy $100-120.

Heritage Hall

Heritage Hall bread and butter plate $4-6, salad plate $10-12, dinner plate $12-15, cereal bowl $8-10, cup/saucer $6-8.

Heritage Hall covered vegetable $60-70, large platter $40-45, small platter $20-25, oval vegetable $20-25, sauceboat $20-25, salt and pepper $30-35 pair, covered butter $35-40.

Heritage Hall teapot $90-100 coffeepot $90-100, creamer $15-18, covered sugar $20-25.

Jolie

Jolie pink. Small platter $22-25, dinner plate $15-18, salad plate $10-12.

Merry Christmas

Merry Christmas sauceboat $50-60, cup/saucer $18-20, square salad $30-35, buffet plate $30-35, mug $22-25, sugar (missing lid) $35-40, square hostess plate with cup $35-40.

Merry Christmas turkey platter $180-200.

Merry Christmas buffet plates. Plate on left is new. Old plates $30-35 each.

Merry Christmas coaster in original box. Coasters $10-12 each.

Merry Christmas backstamp.

Merry Christmas punch set. Bowl $200-225, mugs $20-25 each.

Mill Stream

Mill Stream blue salad plate $12-14, dinner plate $18-20, individual coffeepot $125-150, demitasse creamer $25-30.

Mill Stream pink small platter $50-60, salad plate $14-16, dinner plate $20-25, creamer $30-35.

Mount Vernon

Mount Vernon platters. All with same view from different distance. Small $50-60, medium $75-85, large $100-110.

The Old Mill

The Old Mill brown oval vegetable $20-25, dinner plate $15-18, bread and butter plate $4-6, fruit bowl $6-8, coaster $5-6, cup/saucer $8-10.

Olde English Countryside

Olde English Countryside brown sauceboat $40-45, liner $25-30, small platter $45-50, medium platter $60-70, large platter $90-100.

Olde English Countryside brown demitasse coffeepot $125-140, demitasse creamer $30-35, demitasse saucer $35-40, coffeepot $125-135, sugar $35-40, creamer $25-30.

Olde English Countryside brown 9" square vegetable $40-45, 10" square vegetable $50-60, chop plate $100-110, milk pitcher $60-65, tureen $175-200.

Olde English Countryside brown 9" continental rim soup $18-20, 10" rim vegetable $40-45, 8" rim soup $18-20.

Olde English Countryside blue dinner plate $18-20.

Olde English Countryside brown cup/saucer $15-18, square salad plate $18-20, round salad plate $12-15, dinner plate $18-20.

Olde English Countryside pink dinner plate $18-20.

The Road Home

The Road Home milk pitcher $50-60.

The Road Home dinner plate $15-18.

Rose Bouquet

Rose Bouquet cup/saucer $12-15, dinner plate $18-20, coffee mug $18-20, cereal bowl $12-15.

Rose Bouquet oval vegetable $35-40, round vegetable $35-40, small platter $45-50, sauceboat $35-40.

Strawberry Fair

Strawberry Fair sauceboat $50-55, creamer $40-45, small platter $60-70, large platter $125-150, oval vegetable $50-60, round vegetable $50-60.

Strawberry Fair square salad plate $30-35. dinner plate $30-35, cup/saucer $18-20, double eggcup $35-40

Tally Ho

Tally Ho turkey platter $300-325.

Tally Ho cup/saucer $20-25, small platter $90-100, buffet plate $40-45, fruit bowl $15-18, coaster $15-20

Toile de Jouy, Pastorale

Toile de Jouy, Pastorale. Pink creamer $30-35, dinner plate $18-20, liner $20-25, sauceboat $40-45.

Winchester sauceboat $45-50, liner $30-35, chop plate $120-130, handled cake $130-150, waste bowl $60-70, covered sugar $50-60.

Toile de Jouy, Pastorale. Purple cup/saucer $18-20, dinner plate $22-25, bread and butter plate $8-10.

Winchester dinner plate $30-35, salad plate $20-22, bread and butter plate $10-12, cup/saucer $18-20.

Winchester

Winchester sauceboat with liner $75-85, medium platter $100-120, round vegetable $60-70, oval vegetable $60-70.

Winchester fruit bowl $12-15, rim soup $18-20, dinner plate $30-35, cup/saucer $18-20

146

Windsor Fruit

Windsor Fruit fruit bowl $8-10, salad plate $12-15, rim soup $18-20, bread and butter plate $7-9, oval vegetable $40-45, tab cereal $4-16.

Mason's

Bow Belles

Bow Belles brown salt and pepper shakers $45-50 pair.

Chartreuse

Chartreuse small Hydra jug $90-100.

Chartreuse butter pat $22-25, large octagonal vase $125-140.

Fountains

Fountains pink sauceboat and liner $75-90, creamsoup and liner $35-40.

Fruit Basket

Fruit Basket dinner bell $50-60, octagonal tea caddy $125-135, lunch plate $22-25, Hydra jug $90-100, toast rack $100-115.

Leeds

Leeds square cake plate $90-100, lunch plate $20-22, cup/saucer $15-18, bread and butter plate $8-10.

Manchu

Manchu blue single eggcup $25-30, teacup/saucer $15-18, dinner plate $18-20, salad plate $12-15, rim soup $15-18, creamsoup and liner $25-30, coffee cup/saucer $15-18

Manchu blue creamer $25-30, milk pitcher $65-75, covered sugar $35-40, medium platter $75-85, round vegetable bowl $35-40, relish $20-25.

Manchu green fast-stand gravy $35-40, medium platter (under tureen) $40-45, soup tureen $175-200, large platter $65-75.

Manchu green 8" salad plate $12-15, 10½" buffet $20-25, 9" lunch plate $18-20, 10" dinner plate $18-20, rim soup $10-12.

Manchu green square cake $60-70, 13" chop plate $60-70, round vegetable $35-40.

Manchu green (no tinting) salad plate $12-15.

Manchu pink dinner plate $18-20.

Mandalay

Mandalay cigarette holder $45-50, Hydra jug $90-100, square ashtrays $18-20 each.

Regency

Regency demi-tasse cup/saucer $22-25.

Paynsley Patt

Regency fan-shaped teapot $160-175, Fenton jug $85-95.

Paynsley Patt rim fruit $8-10, lunch plate $18-20, salad plate $12-15, creamsoup and liner $30-35, cup/saucer $15-18, coupe soup $12-15, creamer $25-30.

Ships

Ships. Golden Lion (left), Tiger (right) $30-35 each.

Strathmore

Strathmore footed dragon bowl $150-160.

Stratford

Stratford pink teapot $140-160, rim soup $18-20, covered sugar $35-40.

Stratford blue/grey medium platter $45-50, large platter $60-70, round chop plate $75-85.

Watteau

Watteau brown celery dish $45-50, small Hydra jug $90-100.

Watteau pink tea tile $100-110, Fenton jug $125-140.

Watteau purple Fenton jug $125-140, medium platter $120-130,
small platter $75-85, relish $40-45.

Watteau purple large round vegetable $65-75, small round
vegetable $55-65, handled oval vegetable $75-85,
creamsoup and liner $35-40.

Watteau pink tureen with liner and ladle $550-600.

Meakin

Americana

Americana dinner $12-15, dessert $6-8, cereal $10-12, cup/saucer $6-8.

Americana round vegetable $22-25, platter $25-30, coffeepot $90-100.

Americana catalogue advertisement.

Fairwinds

Fairwinds coaster $5-6.

Fairwinds brown cereal $5-7, dinner $6-8, lunch plate $10-12, fruit $4-6.

Romantic England

Romantic England pink creamer $30-35, dinner plate $22-25, salad plate $20-22, cup/saucer $15-18.

Midwinter

Landscape

Landscape blue rim fruit bowl $15-18, small platter $75-85, salad plate $18-20, rim soup $18-20, demitasse cup/saucer $35-40.

Landscape blue partial Canterbury set. Side sections $45-50 each. Covered $90-100.

Landscape brown multi-color supper set. Complete $180-200. Sides $25-30 each. Covered center serving dish $70-80.

Rural England

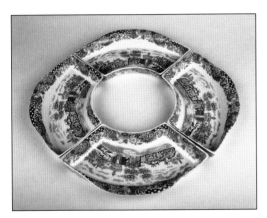

Landscape brown multi-color dinner plate $30-35.

Rural England pink cereal $15-18, salad plate $18-20, coffeepot $150-175, Dutch jug $75-85, cup/saucer $18-20, covered sugar $45-50.

Landscape pink partial supper set. Side sections $25-30 each.

Landscape blue 3-part rectangular relish $120-140.

Rural England blue sugar shaker $110-120.

Myott

Bermuda

Bermuda AD coffeepot $160-175, teapot $160-175,
demitasse cup/saucer $22-25.

Bermuda double eggcup $30-35, buffet plate $30-35.

Country Life

Country Life blue dinner plate $12-15.

Country Life pink rim soup $12-15, coffeepot $85-95.

Palissy

The Hunter

The Hunter pink dinner plate $18-20, blue medium platter $45-50, black salad plate $12-14, black coffeepot $125-150.

Royal Mail

Royal Mail blue chop plate $50-60. Not pictured: dinner plate $12-14.

Avon Scenes

Avon Scenes pink oval sandwich tray $100-125, small platter $50-60, handled cake plate $80-90, covered butter/cheese $75-95, fast-stand sauceboat $75-85, salt/pepper on tray $60-70.

Avon Scenes pink coffeepot $160-175, demitasse coffeepot $125-145, teapot $160-175, creamer $30-35, covered sugar $40-45.

Avon Scenes pink 9¾" round vegetable $45-50, 9" round vegetable $40-45.

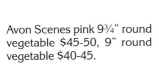

Avon Scenes (Cont.)

Avon Scenes pink cup/saucer $15-18, dinner plate $18-20, salad plate $12-14, rim soup $18-20, single eggcup $25-30.

Thames River small milk pitcher $75-85, large milk pitcher $100-110, coffeepot $160-175, creamer $30-35.

Thames River Scenes

Thames River Scenes blue creamsoup $25-30, dinner plate $18-20, salad plate $12-14, rim soup $18-20, cup/saucer $15-18.

Thames River Scenes blue oval sandwich tray $100-125, small platter $50-60, handled cake plate $80-90.

Thames River pink rim soup $18-20, dinner plate $18-20, small platter $50-60, teacup/saucer $15-18, coffee cup and saucer $18-20. creamsoup and liner $30-35, small tray $18-20, salad plate $12-14.

Royal Staffordshire

Jenny Lind

Jenny Lind pink oval vegetable $45-50, round vegetable $60-70.

Jenny Lind brown multi-color fast-stand sauceboat $60-75.

Jenny Lind pink salad plate $18-20, dinner plate $30-35, cup/saucer $18-20, rim soup $15-18.

Spode

Safe Harbor

Safe Harbor purple round vegetable $50-60, bread and butter plate $12-15, salad plate $18-20, cup/saucer $15-20.

Aster

Aster dinner plate $35-40, cup/saucer $20-25.

Salvation Army

Salvation Army blue dinner plate $12-14, dessert plate $8-10, cereal $6-8, cup/saucer $6-8.

Bouquet

Bouquet large tureen with ladle and liner $550-650.

Bouquet 9" square luncheon plate $30-35.

Bouquet dinner plate $30-35.

Buttercup

Buttercup dinner $22-26, relish $30-35, double eggcup $30-35.

Camilla pink dinner plate $30-35, cranberry bowl $60-65.

Camilla

Camilla blue handled cake plate $90-100, rim soup $18-20.

Camilla teal butter pat $22-25.

Camilla pink infant warming dish $130-150.

Christmas Tree (old mark) butter pat $22-25.

Camilla blue salt and pepper shakers $90-100 pair.

Camilla backstamp.

Spode Christmas Tree (old mark) medium platter $100-125.

Cowslip

Cowslip teapot $160-175, small platter $90-100, oval vegetable $50-60, creamer $30-35.

Cowslip dinner plate $22-25, salad plate $18-20, bread and butter $8-10, cup/saucer $15-18, fruit bowl $8-10, butter pat $22-25.

Fair Haven

Fair Haven dinner $30-35, sandwich plate $18-20, bread and butter $12-15.

Fair Haven handled cake $100-120, small platter $75-95, medium platter $100-120.

Fairy Dell

Fitzhugh

Fairy Dell lunch plate $22-25, salad plate $18-20, dinner plate $30-35, cup/saucer $18-20.

Fitzhugh blue salad plate $30-35, bread and butter plate $18-20, Canton-style cup/saucer $25-30.

Fitzhugh blue regular cup/saucer $22-25.

Fairy Dell creamer $40-45, platter $120-130, oval vegetable $65-75.

Fitzhugh blue covered jug $120-140, milk pitcher $120-130, covered sugar $60-70, teapot $200-225.

Fitzhugh (Cont.)

Fitzhugh blue oval vegetable $90-100, handled octagonal cake plate $140-160, covered vegetable (missing lid) $100-110 (with lid $200-225)

Fitzhugh green coffeepot $200-225, covered sugar $60-70, high handled creamer $65-75.

Gainsborough

Gainsborough large teapot $160-170.

Fitzhugh rust covered temple jar $225-275.

Gainsborough butter pat $22-25.

Greek blue salad plate $20-25, brown butterpat $20-22.

Greek

Greek pink dinner plate $30-35, salad plate $20-22.

Mayflower

Mayflower dinner plate $30-35, salad plate $25-30.

Spode Mayflower

This is one of Spode's early engravings and is typical of the dignified elegance of 18th Century England. The border design, in a delicate shade of Chinese puce, shows the influence of France and Italy. The rose, beautifully painted by hand, is purely English. The Gadroon shape was modelled from English silver of the period. Mayflower is particularly appropriate for the Traditional styles.

ITEMS REGULARLY CARRIED IN STOCK

Plates 10" (Dinner)	Baker 8" (Open Vegetable Dish)
Plates 8½" (Breakfast or Luncheon)	Baker 9" (Open Vegetable Dish)
Plates 7" (Tea or Salad)	Baker 10" (Open Vegetable Dish)
Plates 6" (Bread and Butter)	Sq. Scallop 8" (Open Fruit or Salad Bowl)
Individual Ash Trays (Butters)	Sq. Scallop 9" (Open Fruit or Salad Bowl)
Rim Soups 8"	Covered Dish 10" (Vegetable Dish)
Rim Soups 7"	Sauce Boat Fast Stand (Gravy)
Oatmeal Saucers 6"	Covered Sauce Tureen and Stand
Fruit Saucers 5"	Covered Soup Tureen and Stand 11"
Square Dessert Plates	Pickle Dish
Tea Cups and Saucers	Tea Bowl 36s
After Dinner Cups and Saucers	Teapot No. 1 (8 cups) (Regular)
Cream Soup Bowls and Stands	Covered Sugar No. 2 (Regular)
Square Cake Plate	Covered Sugar No. 3 (Individual Size)
Dish 10" (Meat Platter)	Cream No. 1 (Large)
Dish 12" (Meat Platter)	Cream No. 2 (Regular)
Dish 14" (Meat Platter)	Cream No. 3 (Individual Size)
Dish 16" (Meat Platter)	Coffee Pot 18's (8 cups)
Round Chop 12" (Round Platter)	Joke Cup and Saucer
Round Chop 14" (Round Platter)	

1940s catalogue page for Spode's Mayflower.

Reynolds

Reynolds small teapot $175-195, demitasse cup/saucer $35-40.

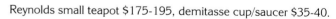

Reynolds sugar bowl $50-60, dinner plate $30-35, creamsoup and liner $35-40.

Rosebud Chintz

Rosebud Chintz bread and butter plate $15-18, sandwich plate $18-20, dinner plate $35-40, double eggcup $35-50, cup/saucer $20-25.

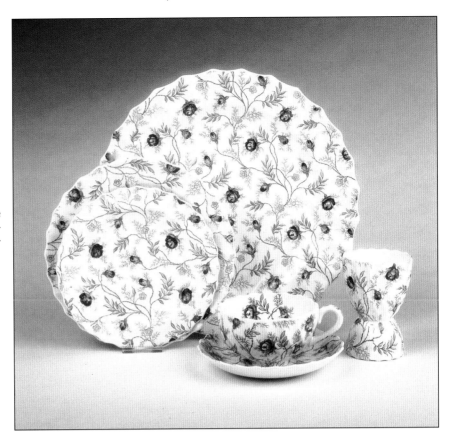

Rosebud Chintz handled cake plate $120-130, creamer $50-60, coffeepot $190-220.

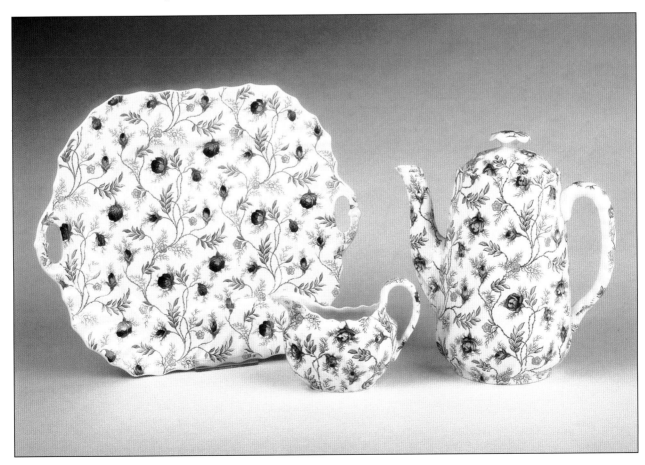

Wedgwood

Ferrara

Ferrara plum rim soup $18-20, salad plate $18-20, dinner plate $30-35, creamsoup/liner $35-40, single eggcup $30-35, cup/saucer $18-20, fruit bowl $12-15.

Ferrara plum oval vegetable $65-75, medium platter $120-130, small platter $75-90, fast-stand sauceboat $75-90, round vegetable $65-75.

Ferrara plum covered
vegetable $160-175,
soup tureen $550-650.

Ferrara plum creamer $40-45, handled cake plate $100-120, coffeepot $175-195, covered sugar $50-60.

Ferrara blue round salad
bowl $200-225.

173

Landscape

Landscape blue rim soup $20-25, oval vegetable $75-85, Dutch jug $100-120, demitasse coffeepot $200-225, saucer $6-8.

Wood & Sons

Hyde

Hyde rim soup $18-20, dinner plate $22-25, salad plate $18-20, bread and butter plate $8-10, cup/saucer $15-18, fruit bowl $8-10.

Woodland

Woodland blue rim soup $15-18, pink salad plate $12-14, pink dinner $18-20, blue salad plate $12-14, blue demitasse creamer $30-35.

Hyde covered vegetable $120-130, small platter $60-70, large platter $130-150, relish/liner $30-35, creamer $30-35, covered sugar $40-45

Bibliography

Coe, Debbie and Randy. *Liberty Blue Dinnerware. Atglen,* Pennsylvania: Schiffer Publishing, 2003.

Copeland, Robert. *Spode*. Buckinghamshire, England: Shire Publications Ltd., 1998.

Finegan, Mary J. *Johnson Brothers Dinnerware Pattern Directory and Price Guide,* Second Edition. Boone, North Carolina: Minor's Printing Company, 2003.

Neale, Gillian. *Miller's Blue and White Pottery: A Collector's Guide*. London, England: Miller's, a division of Mitchell Beazley, imprints of Octopus Publishing Group Ltd., 2000.